ONE | ONE | FIVE

Paperback edition first published in 2011

Published by

A.K.A. Publishing Pty Limited

303 Edgecliff Road
Woollahra 2025
Sydney, Australia

PO Box 2135
Strawberry Hills
NSW 2012
Australia
Phone: +61 02 9326 1499
Fax: +61 02 9362 4385
Email: admin@akapublishing.com.au
Web: www.akapublishing.com.au

ISBN 978-0-9804531-6-4

Cover design by Tracey Gibbs

Research by Alice McClymont

Printed by Griffin Press

ONE | ONE | FIVE

ALAN MANLY, JULIAN DAY & GRAEME BROSNAN

This is a true story.
For privacy reasons some names have been changed and some alterations made to the chronology of events to simplify the narrative.

"When there are too many policemen there is no liberty.
When there are too many soldiers there is no peace.
When there are too many lawyers there is no justice."

Lin Yutang, Chinese writer, 1895-1976

CHAPTER ONE

THE POLICE STATION

You can leave a hand grenade in a baby's pram, or rolling about in the bottom of a fishing boat without a worry in the world. Grenades can be perfectly harmless, until you pull the pin. Remove the safety pin and a spring-loaded striker ignites a four-second fuse. Hurl the thing and your enemies will be blown to smithereens. However, timing is everything. Dither and you will be history. Throw it too quickly and your adversary will pick it up and throw it back. That's the thing with bombs. Although easy to detonate, they're not precise weapons and they're unpredictable as well as deadly.

Late on Thursday afternoon, 8 March 1994, my colleague and friend, Julian Day, walked into North Sydney Police Station with a piece of paper as lethal as a hand grenade and set in motion a chain of events which changed our lives forever. Julian approached the service counter at the station and asked to speak to one of the detectives. The constable serving him enquired, "What's this about?" Julian opened his briefcase and pulled out a single piece of paper. "I am here in my capacity as an office bearer of ITSA, the Information Technology Society of Australia."
"Yes?"
"A not-for-profit organisation."
"Right."

"And this," he said, waving the piece of paper much like Chamberlain did after his meeting with Hitler in Munich, "is an invoice, an outrageous invoice."
"For?" asked the copper, trying to grab the piece of paper.
"Photocopying."
"No, I meant how much is it for?
"One hundred and fifteen dollars," Julian replied.
"Come again?"
"One, one, five," Julian spelled out, barely concealing his rage.
"One hundred and fifteen dollars?"
"Exactly."

The constable took hold of the piece of paper and looked at it. Sure enough, it was a bill for $115. He then gave Julian the once-over. In his late thirties, Julian spoke with an unmistakeable English accent. Certainly he looked sane and was respectably dressed in a suit, but you can never tell.
"And so what do you want us to do?" asked the copper.
"Get on to it. Investigate."
"You want the NSW Police to carry out an investigation because you were lumbered with a bill for $115 for photocopying?"
"Well, yes," Julian agreed. "It's a fraud."

This little pantomime went on for a while between the two, looking back and forth at the piece of paper, with Julian getting the definite feeling that he wasn't very welcome and wasn't going to get far. The constable then gave him a lecture about the serious lack of police resources, the burgeoning crime rate and the fact that the police had better things to do than investigate people for a dispute over a rather piddling amount of money. To the copper's surprise, Julian wasn't going anywhere. "The amount in question is irrelevant," he explained. "The fact is that this invoice is a forgery. And I can prove it."

The man behind the desk was on the brink of simply telling Julian to clear off, but there was something about him, something ridiculous, almost schoolboyish, like a kid reporting that someone had let down the tyres of his bicycle. "Look, I'll tell you what I'll do, mate," said the copper patronisingly. "Now that you've told me everything in full living colour — twice — I'll put it in the Day Book. Okay?"
"The Day Book?"
"Best I can do for you, I'm afraid. We'll stick it in the Day Book. That is an official record of the NSW Police Force which attests to the fact that you have fulfilled your civic duty as an upstanding citizen and reported this fellow. Who knows, in the future people may very well come down here and check the Day Book before they have any photocopying done." A smart arse. What could Julian do? Clearly the police were not interested in his case. Reluctantly, he agreed with the idea of writing an entry in the Day Book on the police station counter.

The copper opened this massive tome which was about the size of the Domesday Book, pulled a pen from his pocket and spoke as he wrote, "Fraudulent invoice. $115." Then he looked at Julian and asked, "And your name is?"

"Day. Julian Day."
"And what's this other chap's name?"
"Lurie. Elliott Lurie," was Julian's reply.
"Lurie, Elliott." The copper's pen was about halfway through the name when it suddenly stopped dead in its tracks. For a brief moment the policeman froze. He looked up from his Day Book. The expression on his face changed completely.
"Did you say Elliott Lurie?"
"That's right."
"How do you spell it?"
Julian spelled out the name. Obviously the cops weren't the world's greatest spellers.
"Take a seat, Mr…?"
"Day."
"Yes, Day, of course. Take a seat, Mr Day. I won't be long."
"But I thought you just wanted to…" Before Julian could finish, the young constable was gone.

It was at this point that Julian remembered what I had told him. "Pay the $115," was my advice. "Pay up. That'll get rid of Lurie and we can forget about the whole thing."
"Oh no," said Julian, "I'm going to the police."
"Mate, be careful. My brother's a cop and they don't appreciate people coming in whinging about the neighbour's cat pissing on their pot plant." But there was no moving Julian once his mind was made up. "You're a director of ITSA, Alan. You have to back me." My final words to him before he toddled off to the police station were, "Just make sure you don't end up being arrested instead for creating a public mischief."

THE POLICE STATION

Down the vast hallway of North Sydney Police Station, Julian could hear a group of policemen talking and their voices seemed to becoming louder and more animated. He heard someone say, "Right! Bring him in." Julian's stomach flipped. Perhaps this wasn't such a good idea after all. If he just picked up his briefcase and bolted from the station, what could they do? He turned and started for the door. "Don't run," he said to himself, "that's a sure sign of guilt. Walk briskly and with dignity out of the station." Julian had only taken a few steps when a detective appeared at the front counter. "Mr Day, is it?" he asked, flashing Julian a huge, friendly smile.
"Yes?"
"Could you come this way, please."

Julian followed the detective upstairs. They walked past various work stations where there were police in uniform as well as some in plain clothes chatting, or typing on keyboards, or talking on the phone. The detective stood at the door of an office and motioned Julian to go in. "Take a seat," the detective said. Julian sat down. He put his briefcase on his lap. Ominously, the detective didn't take a seat himself, but stood at the back of the room. Then in the door came more detectives as well as several uniformed officers with lots of stars and crowns and stripes displayed on their epaulettes. Poor old Julian started to panic. "Look," Julian said apologetically, "I didn't mean to cause you fellows any trouble."
"No trouble at all, Mr Day," barked the heavily braided officer who had a smoothly shaved head. This officer then

went around the room and introduced everyone, but Julian was too intimidated to remember any of their names. With the introductions out of the way a silence descended on the office. They all looked at Julian. Their eyes locked on to him and he was acutely aware they were intensely observing and evaluating his facial expressions and reactions. Notebooks came out, the door was shut, and the questions started.

"Apparently," said the officer who seemed to be in charge, "you've got problems with someone."
"Yes. Elliott Lurie."
The officer with the shaved head leaned in close. "We are very interested in Mr Lurie." He turned and looked at his police colleagues, all of whom were nodding their heads in agreement. "Please tell us more, Mr Day. What does he look like?"
"Look like? Gee. Agh. Well, hard to say. Average height, average build; dark, wavy hair; wears very thick glasses."
The police looked at each other. "That's him all right," one of the detectives remarked.
"He's very…the word 'nondescript' is most apt," Julian added.
"Does he live at Room 23, 66 Riley Street, Lavender Bay?" someone wanted to know.
"Yes, that's right. In a boarding house," Julian agreed.

The smile on the officer's face with the shaved head switched from his plastered-on public relations grin to one of unmistakeable joy. Everyone seemed to relax. There was a brief tap on the door and then in came an attractive young female constable carrying a tray of coffee mugs and a packet of biscuits. Mugs were distributed, milk and sugar offered up and the assorted creams passed around. As Julian munched on a biscuit surrounded by his new best friends he wondered what their interest in Lurie was. The guy must be a serial killer. "And so tell me, Mr Day," one of the detectives enquired, "how did you get tangled up with Lurie?"

CHAPTER TWO

THE BIRTH OF ITSA

I was working at the Statewide Business College where my business partner, Mark Gatehouse, and I were churning out large numbers of competent computer professionals. We had polished up the image of the college which prompted an influx of international students. Naturally, they excelled at mathematics so we guided them into computer programming courses.

Back then, the only computer industry exam that the Immigration Department and employers accepted was one set by the Australian Computer Society. ACS ran exams once a year and as we were one of the best colleges in Australia, many of our students sat the ACS exam. However, many in the computer industry believed that ACS had become too set in its ways. It had been the national industry body for over thirty years during which time there had been a series of IT booms. Every time there was a boom their membership climbed regardless of what they did as an organisation. As a result they had become a little too complacent and took their members for granted. The one good thing ACS had was their annual accreditation exam. Then, in a moment of sublime idiocy, ACS decided to stop running exams altogether. That left organisations like the Statewide

Business College out in the cold because without their exam we didn't have any suitable accreditation system.

Mark Gatehouse and I had a meeting with ACS to resolve this impasse which was a complete waste of time. We decided to go and have a drink to discuss our predicament. Whilst we were at the bar, in walked the NSW Chair of ACS, Julian Day. This was the first time I had met him. I was soon to learn that Julian was an habitué of pubs. As we chatted Julian explained that he was very frustrated with ACS. He had hoped to bring about some change, but felt he was hitting his head against a brick wall and had quit in disgust. We sat there on our bar stools feeling deflated after yet another unproductive meeting. Everyone was peeved: "This is madness. The ACS is never going to change." I don't know whether it was the alcohol that egged us on, or just sheer crazy frustration, but someone came up with the idea: "Let's start a new professional computer society." Everybody seemed enthusiastic. The new organisation would set exams and accept our graduates as members of an association that was recognised in the industry.

Julian and I were the main instigators in setting up the new professional society. We realised that we were going into competition with ACS, and would be seen very much as a breakaway group. The media later described us as "disgruntled ex-members" and ACS as "the Old Guard." And so the Information Technology Society of Australia was born. As one of the founders of ITSA Julian believed he could ensure it would be better at supporting IT professionals. Significantly, ITSA was set up as a not-for-profit company with a limited guarantee to protect its directors. It did not have its own offices and instead used facilities provided at no cost by a company called Techware Australasia Pty Ltd. Julian was the Chairman of ITSA and I was appointed Secretary.

We were quite ambitious about ITSA. Julian had some incredible contacts and one of the ideas we came up with to promote it was to have a monthly breakfast meeting with teams of guest speakers debating a suitably controversial topic of the day. This idea was a poor fit for me because I hate breakfast and getting up early is not one of my strengths, either. Julian actually loves getting up early and having breakfast, so for him it was a marriage made in heaven. Breakfasts typically started at seven o'clock. There would be an introduction, followed by the main debate starting at about seven forty-five. It would be all done and dusted so that people would head back to work by nine.

Before long we had a viable membership and became very well known for our lively debates. At the beginning of September 1993, ITSA hosted a breakfast debate for about two hundred people in the ballroom of the Nikko Hotel. We put together a team of three for each side. On the affirmative team — "Censorship on the internet should be controlled" — we had the Reverend Fred Nile from the Christian Democratic Party, and a couple of other speakers whose names I no longer recall. On the negative side were some high-profile debaters led by Robbie Swan, the Eros Association's media director whose job was really to promote pornography. The Chief Censor himself, chaired the proceedings. This was just at a time when the internet was really starting to take off and the issues of pornography, censorship and freedom of speech were highly contentious.

I wasn't particularly good at networking and Julian didn't trust my brutal social skills with prospective members so smartly he placed me on a table at the back of the room. I sat next to Marlene Goldsmith, a delightful, well-educated woman who was a member of the Upper House of the NSW Parliament. With censorship the topic of debate, much of the conversation centred around sex. It fascinated me that no one was interested in talking about censorship and violence, it was always sex. Marlene quite forcefully made the observation that most of the women she knew when taken out on a date felt obligated to give sex in return. "Where were all these poor helpless females when I was younger?" I wondered, but kept my thoughts to myself. Maybe I had tried to pick up the wrong girls. At the end of the debate the pro-censorship team were voted the winners.

Julian sat at the main table doing all the schmoozing. As we had anticipated the debate was a huge success. After it was all over, a man with dark wavy hair and beady eyes framed by thick glasses approached Julian. "Hi, Julian," he said, "my name's Elliott Lurie and I just wanted to congratulate you on a fantastic event." The guy had a distinctive South African accent and came across as being very suave, very polished. "Oh thanks, Elliott," Julian responded. "Yes, it was an entertaining one today."

Lurie went on to say that he was very interested in what ITSA was doing and wanted to become a member. He had extensive experience in IT having at one time headed up the South African operations of one of the biggest computer companies in the world. It so happened that Julian had worked for the same company in the UK. As there were thousands of employees on just about every continent it turned out they didn't know each other when working there. Lurie also mentioned a new software program called Quick-Smart which apparently revolutionised the way companies and organisations managed documents. He believed this program would be very useful for organisations such as ITSA as it made it a much easier way to disseminate information to members through document IDs as well as the electronic distribution of information. It has to be remembered this was happening just as the internet and email communication were in their infancy. His idea was before its time. Elliott Lurie could certainly talk the talk and Julian was genuinely impressed by him. Another idea floated by Lurie was that he thought he might be able to help increase the membership of ITSA substantially. He extolled the visionary virtues of Quick-Smart and believed it would be ideal for marketing our computer society. According to Lurie, we were on the cusp of a new age, the information age, and computers would take us into another IT boom. ITSA was in the right place at the right time and could be a hugely influential and powerful industry organisation. Instead, we were virtually unknown in the industry.

While these ideas were being tossed back and forth, I was

huddled in a corner somewhere writing out a cheque for the caterers. The reality was that ITSA had no money at all and was funded by my business college. We picked up the deficit for the breakfast debate each month which was usually in the order of a thousand bucks. All of us lived in hope that one day a miracle would occur and that ITSA would at least break even. Although it's possible, perhaps even likely, that I was introduced to Lurie, he did not register on my radar at all. And yet this was the moment when he slithered like a snake into our lives which were never to be the same again.

CHAPTER THREE

THE INVOICE

A few days after our breakfast debate, Lurie tried to flog Julian his Quick-Smart software system which had a feature called 'the electronic committee management methodology'. Friends of Lurie's in South Africa had developed Quick-Smart and he was licensed to sell it. He sent Julian a fax which was really nothing more than an advertisement masquerading as a quiz. There were a series of Dorothy Dix questions, such as, "Would your company/organisation like more business?" and "Would you like more information about Quick-Smart?" Julian went tick, tick, tick in all the boxes and faxed it back to Lurie.

Also, Lurie again offered his services to expand our membership base. At the time an individual membership for ITSA was $100 for a year and for corporations $500. Julian told Lurie he would raise his proposal with the executive, but pointed out that the organisation really had no money for such things. At an ITSA executive committee meeting on 28 October 1993, Julian persuaded the committee to agree to offer Lurie a role as an approved agent to sell ITSA membership with a particular focus on corporate membership. Lurie was to act as our agent and because we had no money the only payment he would receive was a thirty per cent commission calculated on every membership he brought in.

Simple. The parties signed an agreement for a joint venture to implement a twelve month ITSA membership marketing strategy. The agreement stipulated that payment was "commission only" and Lurie had to cover all expenses incurred out of his own pocket.

At the time Julian was working at Techware Australasia, a computer company which operated out of a pokey little office on the Pacific Highway in North Sydney. Techware was really starting to take off and everyone was working flat out. One day Julian was told there was a man waiting to see him at reception. It was Lurie. "I just happened to be in the area," he claimed unconvincingly, "and thought I'd pop in and give you an update." He said he had recruited three new members and wanted to know when he would be paid for that. Julian explained that once their membership cheques had been received and cleared, Lurie would be given his 30 per cent commission. That was all well and good except that Lurie was a bit light on financially and wondered if he could get an advance on those commissions. It was pointed out by Julian that if he was paid now and the memberships didn't proceed, Lurie would have to refund the Society which would make it all a bit messy. Lurie argued the toss for a while and in the end left the office.

About a week later the receptionist at Techware Australasia walked into Julian's office and announced, "That creep's here again." Mr Lurie was back. As it happened he was in the area and thought he would pop in. He wanted to let Julian know that his membership efforts were going well and wanted to see if he could be reimbursed for some artwork. Lurie had a flyer designed and the graphic artist wanted $40 for her efforts. Julian explained that being on commission only Lurie was to pay his own expenses. He reacted with some surprise to this and indicated to Julian that it was only fair and reasonable that he be covered for petty expenses. Also, he was a bit short at the moment and he had already paid the artist woman assuming Julian would cover that. A conversation ensued very similar to the one of the previous week and again Lurie left annoyed, but not disheartened. As he headed for the lift he informed Julian that there was tremendous interest in ITSA and new memberships would soon be flooding in.

The next time Lurie called at Techware, Julian pretended he wasn't in the office. A note was left asking for reimbursement of printing costs. Julian rang me. "That Lurie fellow's been badgering me again. He's claimed expenses for printing. The man's a bloody pest."
"How much does he want?" I asked.
"$188.20."
"Pay it," I suggested. "Then he might stop pestering you."
"Are you sure?"
"I'm becoming soft. Just make sure you get an invoice from him and remind him in no uncertain terms that from now on, he will have to fund these costs out of his own pocket." Julian duly coughed up for the printing expenses. It didn't work, of course. Lurie kept calling in, hanging around Julian's office pestering him for expenses on petty things.

Little by little, Lurie ingratiated himself with Julian whom he saw as being a bit of a soft touch. Noticing an unoccupied desk Lurie asked to 'borrow' the desk for an hour or so. Thereafter he would make excuses to come into Techware's offices to use the desk and before long the desk in the corner became 'his'. This grated on Julian who found Lurie becoming more and more of a nuisance. When he heard Julian was about to go to New Zealand, Lurie asked if he could borrow his laptop to do some work on the ITSA memberships. Back then laptops were these great clunky things and incredibly expensive. Feeling sorry for the bloke, Julian caved in and agreed to lend it to him. However, he made it clear he would need to get it back as soon as he returned from New Zealand.

Meanwhile, Julian's boss was becoming increasingly annoyed at this uninvited guest who persistently wasted their time and utilised their resources. When verbal requests did not work, Julian and his boss resorted to sending Lurie a 'cease and desist' letter. He was no longer welcome at the offices of Techware Australasia. And still he didn't go away. Lurie continued to call in unannounced and ask Julian for money. If his motive was to drive Julian crazy he was succeeding.

At a meeting of the ITSA executive committee, the issue of what to do about Mr Lurie was discussed. His efforts to recruit new members had resulted in the grand total of one new member: Lurie himself. And he had been remunerated $33.33 for his own membership. Clearly his membership drive was a complete failure. When challenged about this, Lurie complained that it was very hard to sell corporate memberships despite having made contact with numerous organisations and paid for photocopying of flyers out of his own pocket. It was agreed that Julian would arrange a meeting with Lurie at which he would again spell out the terms of our agreement: that as ITSA had no money the whole exercise had to be self-funding on Lurie's part. He had to cover his own expenses.

They met at the offices of Techware Australasia. Julian handed Lurie a letter bullet-pointing the agreement and then reiterated what the conditions were. When he finished he said, "You understand everything I have said?"
"Yes," agreed Lurie.
Desperate to tick all the boxes and make sure it was crystal clear, Julian then asked a question. Even as the words tumbled from his lips he knew it was a mistake, but it was too late. "Do you have any questions?"
"Well, yes," Lurie replied. "Before our meeting today, I had to pay for using a friend's office equipment and some photocopying. I was hoping…"
"No."
"…that you would cover those…"
"No, no, no."
"…out of pocket costs which were legitimate…"
"Okay, look. Listen to me. This is the last time. Okay?" Julian said, by now a broken man at his wit's end. "On this occasion and this occasion only, the Society is prepared to cover your expenses, as long as they were legitimate expenses and that you can provide supporting documentation."
"I can do that," Lurie agreed.

The following day he arrived at Julian's office and presented him with an invoice, the soon-to-become legendary invoice numbered 458.J44 for total expenses of $473.91. This was not an invoice from Lurie himself, but an invoice on letterhead from a company called BMR. Lurie had circled the part of the invoice which showed that he had spent $115.00 on photocopying. Bold as brass, Lurie then asked, "When can I have a cheque for the $115 owing?" He wanted immediate payment. When Julian looked at the invoice he noticed that it included jobs Lurie had been contracted to do by other employers. He had thrown in all his expenses into the one invoice. The sum allegedly owing by ITSA was a single line item circled in the bill. Julian told Lurie it was a mess and demanded a separate invoice.

The next day Lurie was back with another invoice. "So when will the cheque for $155 be available?" Lurie wanted to know.

Julian was taken aback. "$155? The amount you claimed was one, one, five."

"That's right, but every time I generate a page it costs me $10. One, two, three, four pages; therefore you now owe me an extra $40. $155."

Julian hit the roof. He thought this was preposterous. He had never communicated any authority for such costs to be incurred, and the whole thing was outside the original agreement to pay him on a commission-only basis. Julian informed Lurie he would be paid $115 subject to verification and authorisation by the ITSA committee.

ONE ONE FIVE

After Lurie left, Julian poured over this second invoice very carefully. Something just didn't look right. It wasn't the amount claimed that looked dodgy, but the invoice itself. The invoice was again on BMR letterhead. It was signed off by Dennis Stanley from BMR and detailed a photocopying component of $115. Then, Julian noticed it had the same reference number as the previous invoice, 458.J44. Legally, this was a huge no-no. It could not be another invoice and yet have the same reference number. Julian then rang the telephone number for BMR listed on the letterhead and asked to speak to Dennis Stanley. However, Stanley was away on holidays. If he was away during the time he had supposedly signed off on the invoice, then Lurie's invoice was a fraud. It was becoming uglier by the second.

Julian called a committee meeting and we discussed the situation. Ever the pragmatist, I said we should pay the bastard and get rid of him. Julian composed a very stern letter and another meeting with Lurie was arranged. This time there were the three of us present. Without any fanfare, Julian read his letter word for word: "As I have stated to you on several occasions, it was never intended nor implied that unauthorised expenses would be funded by the Society. The arrangement we agreed to was that you would sell ITSA memberships and receive a commission equal to thirty per cent of the membership paid. Already you have gone outside the spirit of our arrangement in claiming expenses such as reimbursements for telephone calls, printing and photocopying. To date there has only been one membership sale and you have retained in toto that entire membership fee.

Simple arithmetic will show that the Society cannot afford to conduct its membership drive in this manner." Julian was like a schoolboy stamping his feet. It seemed to make him feel better, but really in these circumstances he was powerless. After a brief pause he resumed, "The Society has not only honoured, but exceeded its requirements. The executive of the Society have approved an ex-gratia payment of $115.00 to cover your expenses as claimed. This payment is made in good faith and as an ex-gratia gesture only. This is not a precedent creation nor is it an admission of liability for future or past expenses."

After he finished Julian handed the letter and the attached cheque over to Lurie. He stared at us both for a moment in that dead-eyed way of his, then ripped the cheque into little pieces, turned on his heel and walked off with what little dignity he could muster. At that moment I knew Lurie was odd, but it never occurred to me that I was about to be his victim. Although in my early forties, I was but a babe in the woods. I deluded myself into believing I was an astute judge of character, that the rational, the logical and the sane triumphed, and that at the end of the day commonsense prevailed. "Thank God we've seen the last of that smart arse," I remarked to Julian confidently. Honestly, I thought it would end right there. Julian was sitting in his chair carefully wiping his nose with a large handkerchief. "What do you think?" I asked.
"Honestly," he sighed, "the man's an imbecile."

It occurred to me that I really didn't know much about Julian. Apart from our dealings with ITSA, I hardly ever saw him. He was a few years younger than me and hailed from Henley-on-Thames, which is famous in the world of rowing for the Royal Regatta. I knew he liked a beer and had been expelled from school for conduct unbecoming of a gentleman. Henley-on-Thames Grammar School occupied a magnificent three-storey building from the 1600s. On the roof there was a bell tower and a rope which hung all the way down through the building. Each day a boy would ring the bell for assembly. Julian decided to climb up on the roof one night and muffle the bell so it wouldn't ring and he would have the perfect excuse for not fronting up to the headmaster's tiresome assembly. To carry out his prank, he gathered together lots of rags, cotton wool and rope and climbed up on to the roof. As he was wrapping rags around the clapper, it accidentally came off and then he dropped it. The clapper fell three storeys down the flue making this 'dong, dong, dong' racket all the way down. Incredibly, no one heard any of this, but he thought it best to get off the roof and head home. Unfortunately, the quickest way home was past the school swimming pool and as he was making his way along the path, Julian remembered that the headmaster often swam there of a morning. What fun it would be for the headmaster to dive into an empty pool. And so under a manhole cover at the deep end he opened a valve which drained the water out of the pool. After an exciting night's work, he ran home feeling rather pleased with himself.

Naturally, the next morning, all hell broke loose. What

Julian hadn't realised was that when the clapper from the bell dropped down the flue it crashed into the fireplace in the headmaster's office which was directly below. The clapper hit the fireplace with such force that it exploded ash and embers in every direction. It looked like Pompeii the day after Vesuvius erupted. Everything in the headmaster's office was covered in a thick layer of ash and embers had left burn marks on chairs, carpets and desks. It was considered a miracle that the place had not burned down. And it didn't end there. The water from the swimming pool had gone down the hill and flooded some new school tennis courts. The headmaster was not at all happy and before long Julian confessed to being the culprit and was expelled.

I thought of Julian as Billy Bunter, the comic book English public schoolboy anti-hero. It was like he'd walked right out of the pages of Billy Bunter: overweight, be-spectacled, pathologically self-centered, snobbish and conceited, perpetually with his hand out trying to raise a loan, but witty and charming. All the elements of a good salesman.

After school he did a stint at one of the big four computer companies, and then worked for Oxford University Press, the book publishers, where he set up a brand new warehouse and distribution centre for them. That whetted his appetite for software development which he did at Phillips until he fell in love with an Adelaide girl, backpacking through Europe. She persuaded Julian to follow her back to Australia. Once here he went straight into a start-up company, Cortex Pacific, as the sales and marketing director. They signed up big companies like Lend Lease, Coca-Cola and BHP.

When he had been working in the UK, Julian was a member of the British Computer Society and not long after arriving here transferred his membership across to the Australian Computer Society which is where I first met him. Julian felt that the ACS was a very poor cousin of the British Computer Society and needed to be shaken up. After being elected to the branch executive he started a push for change, but after several years came to the conclusion it wasn't worth the effort.

At ITSA our efforts to establish a credible alternative to ACS were being railroaded by the time we were wasting dealing with Elliott Lurie. Not long after the "tearing up the cheque" incident, Dennis Stanley of BMR came back from leave and returned Julian's call. As Julian had suspected Stanley had been away at the time he supposedly signed off the invoice. In fact he had been overseas and therefore his absence was recorded in his passport. Julian faxed over a copy of the invoice Lurie had presented and his worst suspicions were confirmed. "No," said Stanley, "that is not one of my invoices."
Julian called me. He was livid. "I'm going to the police."
"You are? What for?"
"This invoice is a forgery and he's a criminal."
"He might sue us," I wondered out aloud.
"Nah, as a not-for-profit organisation the maximum liability of the Society cannot be more than $500." We took great comfort in that fact, but I did suggest to Julian that the police may not take kindly to him lodging a complaint.

CHAPTER FOUR

THE MISSING TWO THOUSAND

The officers at North Sydney Police Station were clearly pleased with everything Julian had told them. "We'll need a statement from you detailing all this, of course."

"No problem," Julian replied. There were smiles all round. Having related his story about the mysterious Mr Lurie, Julian asked the rather obvious question, "Why are you so interested in Lurie?" The police looked at one another and then the officer with the shaved head explained the situation.

On Christmas Eve 1993, North Sydney Police Station was a hive of activity. For a lot of businesses it's their biggest day of the year and one of the busiest times of the year for the police. As well as traffic accidents to attend to, there were the usual robberies, muggings, sexual assaults and deaths to deal with. All leave had been cancelled and the phone was ringing off the hook.

This particular afternoon however, there was an aggrieved gentleman on the other end of the line to report a serious robbery. He was staying at a boarding house down near the Lavender Bay wharf in North Sydney and $2,000 of his money had been stolen. A constable was dispatched to investigate.

When the constable arrived the man whose money had been stolen identified himself as Elliott Lurie. He was renting a single room which had a bed, a cheap little side table, a chair and not much else. What had happened, he explained, was that he left $2,000 in cash on the side table and went downstairs to use the communal toilet. When he came back the money was missing. The young constable checked the door lock. "There's no sign of a forced entry. Obviously whoever did this had a key."

"Oh, no," explained Lurie, "the door was open."

The constable was incredulous. "Let me go through this again. You left the cash on that table and the door was open?"

"Yes."

"And you went downstairs, leaving the door open, and $2,000 in cash just sitting there in plain view?"

"Yes."

"And when you came back it was gone?"

"Obviously stolen," Lurie responded.

The constable thought he had heard everything, but this guy really took the cake. "Why would you leave $2,000 stacked up next to your bed, in a boarding house, with the door wide open? You must be a fucking idiot. There must be thirty, forty, fifty people living here. Anyone could have taken that money. For God's sake, do you think the police have got nothing better to do on Christmas Eve than waste their time trying to find money that you should have kept under lock and key?"

The young constable stormed off and headed back to the station. By the time he arrived the shift sergeant was involved. Mr Lurie had taken umbrage at the attitude displayed by the attending police officer and was threatening to make a formal complaint. The sergeant questioned the constable about what had happened and concluded the story as told to him couldn't be true. He and the constable climbed back into the car and returned to the boarding house.

The sergeant, being a man of many years, decided the best approach was a man-to-man chat with this astonishing fuckwit. After hearing the exact same account from the alleged victim, the sergeant used the full, broad and uninhibited vocabulary of the NSW Police to give Lurie an absolute shellacking.

By the time the shift sergeant and the young constable arrived back at their North Sydney headquarters one of the station commanders was caught up in the saga. Lurie had informed him that he had meticulously documented everything that had been said and had every intention in taking legal action against the officers involved. The station commander debriefed his officers and despite all manner of pressing police matters, decided to go and see Lurie and nip the whole thing in the bud.

Back to the boarding house they went. The station commander was very apologetic. He acknowledged that the constable was out of line, but he was overworked, doing long shifts, under a lot of stress, and what have you. And the shift sergeant had been looking at the bigger picture, didn't take into account Lurie's situation personally, and it being Christmas Eve and so forth. It was a classic charm offensive from the top brass. All the ruffled feathers were smoothed down. They shook hands and wished Lurie a merry Christmas. The station commander felt pretty good after their little chat. As far as he was concerned that was the end of the matter.

Any thought that the issue had been amicably resolved evaporated when they arrived back at the station. Lurie had contacted the office of the Police Commissioner and complained that the police had been to his residence three times and yet not one of them had carried out any investigation into the theft of his money. He implied that it was possible the police were in on the theft and as soon as the Christmas break ended, he would lodge a formal complaint with the Police Integrity Commission, the Ombudsman and the Independent Commission Against Corruption. Moreover, he would be taking legal action against all the officers involved from the North Sydney Police Station. Up until this time these officers had had very impressive careers with the police service. They were considered professional, experienced, and clean.

This was a fairly serious state of affairs in anyone's language, but for the police the ramifications were particularly grim. Once a complaint is lodged against an officer at the PIC or ICAC, that officer is automatically excluded from entitlements to promotion or transfer until the matter has been investigated and findings made by the relevant commission. This meant that the careers of all these officers were frozen because of Lurie's complaint.

Of course, what can be forgotten in all this is that there was no actual evidence as to whether Lurie even had $2,000 to his name or, that if he did, he ever left such a sum of money on his bedside table. The police became so caught up in the frenzy of Lurie's attack on them that there was never any investigation into where Lurie ever got hold of $2,000; which account it was withdrawn from, or if it was given to him, who gave him such a sum. In the New Year, he commenced legal action against the other residents of the boarding house, the owner of the building, the security company which sent a patrol past the place once in a blue moon, as well as some workers who happened to be installing fire extinguishers on the day of the alleged theft.

A fireman, who lived down the hallway from Lurie, had no alternative but to hand over $2,000 because he had to have a clean record. The Fire Brigade cannot employ a fireman with a criminal record. People accused of stealing can't be trusted to rush into people's houses or businesses to put out fires. Lurie made such a fuss that the landlord and the security company also paid him compensation. There was just a smell about the whole sordid business.

While the officers at North Sydney were trying to cope with the deluge of enquiries by ICAC, the PIC, as well as the Ombudsman, Lurie made good his threat to sue them personally for negligence for failing to investigate the theft properly, and took action in the District Court. Things were looking decidedly shaky for the coppers when in the door walked one Julian Reginald Day. They were incredibly lucky. As he lived in Drummoyne, Julian had intended reporting Lurie to his local station, but as his office was in North Sydney he decided, on the spur of the moment, to go there instead. Fate sent him to the only station in the country which had ever heard of Elliott Lurie. When Julian walked into North Sydney Police Station claiming he had evidence that Lurie had committed fraud they welcomed him with open arms. Statements were typed and sworn, warrants were issued and as Julian sipped another cup of coffee, a couple of squad cars roared off with sirens blaring to arrest Mr Lurie.

CHAPTER FIVE

THE LAPTOP

When Julian had returned from New Zealand towards the end of 1993, his laptop was still in the possession of one Elliott Lurie. This was after he had demanded his $115 for photocopying, but before Julian had gone to the police. Lurie refused to return the laptop on the basis that his costs had not been paid. He claimed the laptop as a lien against the contract for all the costs he had accrued, or in reality, made up. Not surprisingly, Julian was pissed off with the guy.

After making several reasonable requests for the return of his laptop, Julian started legal action in the Local Court. Someone had told him that the easiest way to retrieve the computer was through the courts: just walk in, get a claim form and serve it on Lurie. Then in time they would be up before a magistrate.

However, serving a summons on Lurie was no easy matter, something that we were to learn time and again over the years. For the uninitiated, I should explain that in just about all courts the world over, certainly in the courts in this country, you can't actually initiate legal action against someone unless the correct court documents have been 'served' on them. To effect service on a person, the defendant must be handed the documents physically and in person. It is no good posting them, or sending a courier; he can deny ever receiving them. The documents must be served on the party concerned and usually a process server is engaged for this task. The process server does actually earn his money because finding someone and serving them is hard work. After that, once legal action is commenced, the lawyers take over. They meet and greet and bond as only they know how, and proceed to transfer wealth from the aspiring middle-class to the more deserving legal elite.

It was at this point in time that Julian and I started to realise that we didn't actually know an awful lot about Mr Lurie. We looked at the ITSA membership records and discovered that despite undertakings he had given, Lurie wasn't actually a member. Then we looked at correspondence he had sent and noticed there were no details as to where his business was located. In short, all we had was a name, and as you would expect there was no public phone and address listing for one Elliott Lurie.

Julian had the patience of a saint and simply bided his time knowing that as a creature of habit, Lurie would one day arrive at his office unannounced and pester him over his unpaid expenses. This is what subsequently happened at which time Julian shook his hand and then said, "Oh, by the way, I am serving you this notice," and handed the stunned Lurie a summons.

The case was heard before a magistrate in the Local Court. Julian represented himself as did Lurie. The magistrate found in favour of Julian and ordered the immediate return of the laptop. Lurie refused to surrender the computer as he announced he would be appealing the finding. The matter then went before the Appeals Court, who dismissed the appeal and directed the matter back to the Local Court. Nine months later the magistrate in the Local Court looked down from the bench and said, "Mr Lurie, give it back." He was also ordered by the court to pay Julian's costs which amounted to a couple of hundred dollars. At this point Lurie explained to the magistrate that he was short on funds that week and asked if he could pay next week. The magistrate relented. Both Julian and Lurie signed the court order and then went to the Registry to get it photocopied and put it on the record. Then Lurie turned to Julian and handed him the laptop.

Even then Julian knew he would never see the court costs Lurie owed him, but he didn't care. He was elated to have at last recovered his laptop and obviously Lurie's sordid association with ITSA was ended. This was an excellent result. We were both feeling very smug at how clever we were in managing to extract ourselves from any involvement with this character who was clearly more trouble than he was worth.

CHAPTER SIX

THE CONVICTION

If only Julian and I had the foresight to see what the next eleven years would bring. If only I had been able to hear a voice in my head say, "Don't do this." We fell head first into a pit so dark and deep, it is a wonder we ever survived to tell the tale. This was the beginning of eleven long, lonely years trapped in a legal abyss.

The fraud case against Lurie was to be heard at the Downing Street Centre. Everyone was there: the commanding officer, the detectives, the shift sergeant, the young constable as well as a team of police prosecutors. I must confess that when I caught sight of Lurie my hackles were raised. The officer with the shaved head noticed this and very wisely had me taken off to a room, which was actually a holding cell. It was quite interesting. The only time I have ever been in a cell. They kept me there and brought me sandwiches and drinks. Two of them sat there with me because I was a witness. I was allowed to go to the toilet, but they would go with me. The police were very keen that nothing go wrong in this case. One of the officers would pop down every now and then and ask, "Everything fine?"

"Just ticketyboo," I responded. "Being a witness is obviously quite something."

"Yes, yes. Don't worry," he said. "The lads looking after you?"
"Oh, yes, they are nice folks."
"We've been talking about the football," one of my minders volunteered.
I didn't have the heart to tell him I hated football.

Finally, I ended up in the courtroom before a female magistrate, Karen Evans-Holt. My first ever experience of being in a courtroom. The prosecutor was also a woman, and believe me she must have been one of the top prosecutors in the country. I was no expert, but it was apparent that the police had thrown amazing resources into this case. Lurie had caused them a lot of pain. They were very passionate and determined to win.

Julian and I gave our evidence. The invoice in question was examined in great detail. One thing that needs to be remembered is that technically Lurie had actually done the work he had claimed. He called it a 'reconstructed invoice'. Lurie typed up the invoice himself and signed it on behalf of the owner of the business which had actually provided the photocopying service. However, the owner of the company was overseas and that was his undoing. It was overwhelmingly obvious that the invoice had been deliberately altered by someone, but the magistrate was wavering. "Well, you know," she said reluctantly, "it could have been a confusion."
"No, no, no," cried the prosecutor.
The magistrate hesitated. She looked down at the

defendant. "Look, Mr Lurie, once a person is convicted of fraud, it is a very serious offence. It is only $115, after all."
"The amount is irrelevant, your Worship," the prosecutor thundered.
"But," wavered the magistrate, "you would have to show intent."
Up went a great wail from those in the court. The prosecutor was having none of it. "We have done that three times," she reminded the magistrate.

Incredibly, the magistrate called Lurie back to the stand and threw him a lifeline. "Now, Mr Lurie. Did you change the document to obtain money from Mr Day and Mr Manly?"
"Of course I did."
"Oh, I give up," the magistrate muttered. She adjourned proceedings and about an hour later we reconvened to hear her decision. In her judgment she noted that it was difficult to say exactly what hours were attributable for the work Lurie had done for ITSA, but the invoice that he presented for payment clearly was an invoice that he knew to be false or misleading in the sense that he knew that it was not an invoice that had been generated by BMR. "The invoice, for $115, was in fact a creation entirely of Mr Lurie," she announced. Her Worship convicted Lurie of making a false statement with intent to obtain money. He was fined $500 and ordered to pay witness expenses of $500 to Dennis Stanley and $2,202 to Julian Day. She allowed him three months to pay.

There is a God. The police and the prosecutor were ecstatic.

There were smiles all around and much shaking of hands. I shot a look over to Lurie. Most people would be upset or distressed being found guilty of a criminal offence like fraud, but it seemed to me from the look on his face that it didn't bother him. It made me think the guy was definitely weird.

Lurie stood up and asked to speak. He informed Her Worship that his intention was to lodge an appeal with the District Court immediately as he was not guilty of fraud. No one really took any notice of him any more. The police knew that their case was watertight and that there really was no avenue of appeal; particularly after Lurie's statement on oath when asked if he had altered the invoice, "Of course I did." His other case against the police where he sued them for negligence was thrown out of court, but in what was to become a trademark of Lurie's modus operandi, curiously the court lodgement fees were not paid and the application for surety of costs by the police was struck out.

Disregarding my natural loathing of public bars, I joined Julian and our new-found friends from the NSW Police for a celebratory drink. The thing with me and Julian is this: if you put the two of us in a room for a couple of hours and let us talk we would find that we had absolutely nothing in common. Our only commonality was the court case. I regard him as a friend, but we have never socialised. He goes to the pub every night whereas I can't stand hotels. Why would I want to stand around and drink beer? Julian goes to everything he is invited to. He loves a party, enjoys meeting complete strangers and networking. Me, I'd sooner die than find myself sipping cocktails and nibbling hors d'oeuvres in a room packed with people I'd never met before. Naturally, the subject of Lurie and his missing money from the boarding house came up. Julian revealed that he had once lived in a boarding house. "Actually," he said, "someone also stole something of mine at that boarding house. A fruit cake."

"A what?" someone asked.

"A fruit cake. Yes. My mother had baked me a fruit cake and posted it to my boarding house. I opened up the package and was delighted. I made a cup of tea, cut off a slice and it was delicious. A short while later I went to the WC. When I came back I pottered around for a bit and then realised my cake had vanished. I couldn't believe it. I looked everywhere, but of course my room wasn't terribly big. Some light-fingered beggar had taken the whole cake. Everything was there — the packaging, the knife, my plate — but no cake. I was furious. I grabbed my coat and went down to the local police station and reported it."

"You didn't!" One of the coppers chipped in.

"I did."

When Julian reported his stolen fruit cake the local constabulary had a great time at his expense. They said they were taking it so seriously they were cancelling all leave for the station and forming an elite task force to investigate. A very detailed description of the cake would be taken and an artist called in to do a sketch. There was also talk of obtaining search warrants for the other rooms in the boarding house as well as bringing in sniffer dogs. In the end, one of the bobbies implied that perhaps Julian was the fruit cake and that he certainly had something missing. At some point during the blur of that evening I made the observation to the assembled drinkers, no doubt showing off, how much like Billy Bunter my friend Julian was. To my surprise, he seemed greatly offended by this.

The next day I returned to the courthouse, the scene of our triumph, and paid fifty bucks or thereabouts for a Certificate of Conviction. If you are a party to the conviction you can purchase the Certificate of Conviction for a small fee. It was something I was going to have framed and displayed on my office wall because more than one solicitor had said to me, "Now that he has been convicted of fraud you will never see him again." People praised Julian and me for showing our mettle and seeing this thing through to the end.

We lived on that for a fortnight. Things were really sailing along. Then, as I was driving up my driveway after a day at the office, I noticed one of those government-issue gold-coloured envelopes sticking out of my letterbox. I ripped it open and found inside a writ from Lurie. He had commenced legal action against Julian and me as directors of ITSA on the basis that we had broken our contractual agreement with him. He sued us for $234,256 plus interest and damages claiming loss of sponsorship, loss of income, breach of contract and negligent management.

CHAPTER SEVEN

BEFORE THE COURT

Lurie appealed Magistrate Evans-Holt's fraud conviction in the District Court and also took action against Julian and me claiming damages. We were District Court file number 7719M of 1994. When I discussed it with a solicitor he said it was a ridiculous claim which would be no effort to defend and be knocked out on the first day. ITSA Limited was set up as a not-for-profit organisation, limited by guarantee. The limitation was $500 per member. We had about six directors, all volunteers, and we were assured by our solicitor who specialised in commercial law that even if everything went horribly wrong for us, the most we would ever be out of pocket was $500. This was the protection afforded by the famous "corporate veil" which separates the corporation from the stockholders as individuals and protects them from being personally liable for a firm's debts and other obligations. Secondly, there was never any contract between Lurie and us. The more our solicitor thought about it, the more he believed we didn't even need him when we went to court. It was really such an open-and-shut case he suggested that Julian and I handle it ourselves. There really was no chance Lurie's claim for damages would ever get up.

On the appointed day, Julian and I faced off against

Lurie in the District Court. He was representing himself and launched into a tirade claiming all manner of dishonesty and negligence on our part. Having been worded up by our solicitor, when it was our turn I stood and explained with great deference to the judge the reasons why this spurious claim should be struck out. To our amazement the judge said he would not be striking out the claim and would now call for further evidence. Noticing the looks of disbelief on our faces he peered over the bench at Julian and me and said, "You fellows had better get yourselves some legal advice."

An adjournment was called and after a frantic phone call to our solicitor we were sent to some barrister's chambers next to the Supreme Court. We trundled up there and someone pointed us in the direction of 'Young Bob' who we were told could possibly help us. We went into Young Bob's chambers. He was an elderly gentleman, about ninety-nine not out. Julian and I sat in these incredibly uncomfortable chairs as Young Bob listened to our story in a casually disinterested sort of way. He thought what had happened to us was terrible. "The structure of ITSA," he opined, "being limited by guarantee, would dissuade a prolonged legal dispute." After seeming to weigh it up in his mind, Young Bob announced with all the solemnity of someone pronouncing the last rites, "Very well, I will do it for you."

Young Bob appeared for us and we were done like a dinner. Lurie was better prepared and made Young Bob look like a complete idiot. Our barrister's strategy was a one shot in the locker affair where he pleaded the same arguments we had. When that failed Young Bob was all at sea. As we were walking back from court, tails between our legs, Young Bob said proudly, "That'll be the last you hear from Mr Lurie. He may have scored a few points, but I've destroyed just about all his options."

Julian and I were stunned. Young Bob thought it was a victory. Talk about spin. People assume that politicians are the masters of spin, but they are nothing compared to the legal profession. "Did you fellows notice," Young Bob added, "how rattled he was when I had him cornered?"
I couldn't resist and shot back, "Just before he turned and ran all over us, you mean?"
"Yeah, about then," Young Bob acknowledged sheepishly. "But, I can tell you from decades of experience, this man won't bother you again. We showed him. If you mess with us we'll wheel in the big guns and destroy you." We shelled out $5,000 for that debacle and were back in court inside a week.

Like all fools Julian and I then did the obvious. We went out and hired a team of solicitors to defend us against Lurie's claim for damages: John Donnelly and Karen Fairburn. When we met with our solicitors and barristers I brought up the fact that this wasn't supposed to happen. Apparently, the so-called corporate veil's protection was not ironclad. If a court determined that business was not conducted in accordance with the provisions of corporate legislation it could hold the directors personally liable. Despite all the assurances that this would never happen in our case, this is exactly what happened. Lurie sued us as individuals and a court allowed him to do that. When the litigious Mr Lurie arrived on the scene the other directors vanished into thin air leaving only Julian and myself. Our new barrister compared the case to a heavyweight championship bout: you only have to win eight out of the fifteen rounds. "Don't let the fact that you lost the other day worry you." Solicitors are trained to do this. No matter what happens, it is always good news.

One of the first problems we encountered was serving documents on Lurie. In breach of the rules of the court, he did not provide a street address for service and instead only listed a post office box. Our legal team assured us that this sort of nonsense was not tolerated by any court in the land. On the appointed day we were sitting outside court and our solicitor came bouncing along, always that traditional five minutes late. Mr Busy was carrying an unsorted sheaf of papers and our barrister began asking for various documents. It soon becomes apparent that Mr Busy was also Mr Disorganised. "It's here somewhere," he wailed as he looked everywhere. My colleague and fellow-defendant, Julian Day, opened his briefcase and magically plucked the right document out. I thought, "Wow and we're not even paying him."

When we took our places in court I noticed that Mr Lurie had no legal team and was representing himself. From somewhere deep within my being came this momentary feeling of sympathy. "Poor bastard," I said to myself. The

first issue raised by our barrister was that of effecting service. Our barrister rose to her feet and complained, "Isn't it a little difficult to serve documents if the man lives in a letter box, Your Honour?" People in the court started sniggering. With a smile on his face the judge replied, "Perhaps Mr Lurie actually resides in a post office box. Is that the case, Mr Lurie?"
"It is, your Honour."
Clearly the judge was not expecting him to say this, but instead of pointing out the absurdity of the situation he ruled that forthwith we had to serve the documents to Lurie in person in a letterbox.

Our barrister railed against this being completely preposterous without effect. Julian and I were reassured this ruling would be overturned and it later was, but for me it was a window into the world of the law where the courts had this unwritten motto, 'Never lose a customer'. I used to tell people that the Latin dictum you saw plastered prominently over every courthouse doorway literally translated as 'Never lose a customer'. Their role was not to secure justice for wronged parties, but to encourage legal action in every way possible. More writs means more matters and more filings and more hearings and more lawyers, judges and court officials, all up to their elbows in well-paid work.

These items of trivia which ultimately have no bearing on the evidence before the court totally occupied our defence team. It seemed to me that it didn't matter what Lurie did, the court always found a way to keep him in the game. On more than one occasion, he simply failed to appear. Here we were, ready to defend ourselves and at considerable expense, and Lurie was nowhere to be seen. Given that he had received notice of the hearing, we asked that his claim be struck out. No, that may be unfair as due to some administrative oversight the hearing had not been listed in that day's edition of the *Sydney Morning Herald.* It was pointed out to the judge that Lurie had failed to appear on other occasions when the hearing had been advertised. "Perhaps he was unwell," someone conjectured. Any excuse, however tenuous, was enough to keep it going. The ruling was that the matter would be stood over to another date.

Each time we went to court, I noticed that we were more organised than our solicitor and that the legal arguments became more puerile and trivial. Our barrister pounded away in an admirable fashion and we got nowhere. Everything we were told couldn't happen, actually happened.

At the same time as all this was happening Julian and I kept a close eye on Lurie's appeal against his conviction for fraud. Obviously, that conviction was a very important weapon in our defence against Lurie and so our legal team attended that hearing. Judge McDonough agreed with the magistrate's original finding and the appeal was dismissed. McDonough ordered that Lurie pay $1,000 to be lodged in recognizance, but he whinged and whined about how he had no money at the moment and couldn't pay.

CHAPTER EIGHT

ALAN PHILLIP JAMES MANLY

It did occur to me that I should change professions, considering what I was going through, but in the end I realised it would be very difficult for me to become a lawyer. It would mean going back to high school. I finished my education in Year 9. Sometimes, I like to tease my wife's educated friends by telling them this: that it wasn't just any Year 9, it was Year 9 Bacchus Marsh High School. It's not a bad line. They usually sit there trying to figure out why they have never heard of my old school.

In a country town in those days there was a state primary school and a Catholic primary, but only the one government high school. We were all streamed A, B, C and D, brightest to dumbest, with the Catholics making up 100 per cent of the D class. True story. This had almost nothing to do with the kids and everything to do with the public primary being more attuned to the public high school, whereas the Catholic school was wasting time teaching things like Latin and Prayers which were absolutely useless in the public high school system.

I was put in the A class and after a term of not too much hard work, I was put into the B class. It was pretty hopeless and I was very disillusioned. My mother didn't value education and my brother David and I were encouraged to leave the moment it was legally possible to do so. We needed the money. The Manlys were very poor, but I guess a lot of people were poor then.

We had a little farm of about eight acres on the outskirts of Bacchus Marsh in the north-west of Victoria. Our father was ill and my brother and I were too young to work the farm. Before my time, during World War II, the Americans set up a military base in Bacchus Marsh. Now can you imagine what happens in a rural town when the Americans arrive? It's been depicted in books and films many times over, but best captured by the quip, "Overpaid, oversexed and over here". The Americans came knocking on Dad's door and wanted eggs, that is eggs by the truckload. My father was no mug. He knew exactly how to deal with these Americans. "They can go to hell," he said, "as if I would ever stoop to sellin' eggs to the bloody Yanks." A weak-willed neighbour succumbed to this earthly temptation of dealing with the foreign soldiers, and lo and behold he became rich. They made more money than they could ever dream of, but even though we were poverty stricken, we had principles. The Americans proved to be an absolute bonanza for all the local farmers, except us.

At one stage Dad built a couple of sheds on the farm. Each one was only eight foot six inches high and they were this height for two reasons: he didn't own a ladder, and he built them singlehanded. He was totally anti-social; a recluse; he did not want people visiting us and as a consequence we could not bring friends home from school. Quite a bright man, my father; he was well read in history and politics to the extent of having read the Greek classics. I was told that he was the single biggest user of the local library.

We lived on eight acres of dirt. Calling it a farm would be considered deceptive under the *Trade Practices Act.* It was barely productive. My father was quite old and unwell. He was about fifty by the time I was born in 1950. When I was about ten years old, he had a heart attack, which was devastating in those days. If you survived, you were an invalid. Dad survived and on that day our world changed from poverty to severe poverty. The farm was sold and we went to live in the town. There was just enough cash for a house, it had to be cash as my parents had no ability to borrow. We existed on a government pension. Obviously, we were poor people. Indeed, we didn't even have a car, which at the time was uncommon in Bacchus Marsh.

This was rural poverty 1960-style. The social security system was then very limited. My family was at the bottom of the socio-economic tree and let me tell you, poverty is not a lot of fun. My parents' greatest hope in the whole world was that my brother and I would get a government job. To them, that was like winning the lottery. If you worked for the government you would have an income and never be unemployed. Even though I was only a boy I could see the alternatives. When I looked over the fence I discovered that our neighbours did far better than us.

I can remember my mother was very annoyed that the ever-interfering government had changed the law and lifted the school leaving age from fourteen to fifteen. My brother left school when he turned fourteen and found a job at the local post office pedalling a pushbike around delivering the mail.

Following the heart attack, my father then suffered a series of strokes and his health just went downhill. During my adolescence, I assisted my mother nursing him. Then when I turned fifteen, my mother insisted that I leave school. However, I wanted to go on with my education. I liked the process of learning and decided to go on into Year 10. The problem was that I didn't have any textbooks. At first I got by through borrowing other kids' textbooks. Finally, I was caught out by the headmaster. At assembly one day it was announced that all the students who didn't have textbooks were to take a form home to fill in to apply for government assistance. My mother wouldn't sign the form and without text books I could not really continue. However, it would be entirely wrong to picture my mother as some sort of provincial philistine. She was a woman of faith and a compassionate person. Before marrying my father she decided to work as a Baptist missionary with the Kanakas on the cane-fields of Central Queensland. Most of the Kanakas had been kidnapped from various Pacific Islands and shipped to the sugar plantations where they were enslaved and treated very poorly. The apparent ill-treatment of the Kanakas appealed to my mother's missionary instinct. By the time she arrived in Queensland it seemed they weren't all that oppressed. No doubt there were plenty of instances of abuse and exploitation, but she found that some of the Kanakas had actually become landowners. And because they were not Aboriginals, they were able to vote and had the same rights as everyone else. The Kanakas were brought in to address a severe labour shortage; the union fight against them which culminated in the infamous White Australia Policy was less about racism and more to do with preventing the country being flooded with cheap labour.

Five years after my brother, I followed the same path, the same steps literally. I was employed by what was then called the Post Master General as a telegram boy. In those days most people did not have a telephone. Urgent news, usually bad news, was delivered by a boy on a pushbike bearing a telegram. You paid by the word and so messages were very succinct: "GRANDFATHER SERIOUSLY ILL STOP COME AT ONCE STOP"; that kind of thing. It was like having an email hand-delivered.

Having successfully mastered those skills, I was promoted to postman. All you had to do was pedal a bike around, shove letters into mail boxes and blow a whistle to let them know the mail had arrived. And there were two deliveries of mail a day: morning and afternoon. Now that was service. Most people looked forward to the arrival of their mail and for many I was the highlight of their day.

However, I did develop a particular dislike for dogs, which I still have; and a bizarre obsession for black socks. On commencement with the PMG we were issued a big, brown box which contained our uniforms. Everything was supplied: shirts, trousers, belts, hats, jackets and bundles and bundles of black socks. In fact, it was the best clothing I had ever worn. Socks were not inexpensive and to have so many pairs was tantamount to luxury in the Manly household. Thereafter, I was emotionally scarred for life. An over-supply of black socks became a benchmark from which there could be no turning back. Over the years girlfriends and wives have stumbled upon boxes and boxes of black socks in my drawers and wondered what kind of nutcase they were dealing with.

The fact that both Manly boys were working for the PMG was seen by Mum as a turning point in the family fortunes. My brother survived as a postman for ten years and then joined the police force. Unlike David, I was soon bored by the whole business. Delivering the mail is tedious in the extreme. One of the few amusements I enjoyed was taking the mail to this old block of council flats where about twenty pensioners lived. When it was pension day I used to deliberately put the cheques in the wrong letterboxes; unit one's cheque in unit two's letterbox, two's cheque in three and so on. Then, I'd blow my whistle. They would come to collect their mail only to discover they had someone else's cheque and I would sit across the road on my bike and watch them arguing and occasionally fighting among themselves. Pathetic, I know, but we were light on for entertainment in Bacchus Marsh.

After about eighteen months I had an unbelievable stroke of

luck. The local television repair man needed an apprentice and offered to take me on. My mother was aghast. At the PMG I was getting $17 a week and if I took up the apprenticeship my income would drop to $13 a week. Why would I throw away one of the best jobs in the world to work for this fellow for less money. She tried to talk my prospective employer out of it, but he was so desperate for people he took no notice. He knew my family circumstances and confided that the apprenticeship papers had to be signed by me and one parent. "Go home and get your father to sign right there." he explained, pointing to a line on the form. "See, I want you to bring this back signed right there."

"Really?"

"Just make sure it is signed right there and we'll send it to the government."

Even I cottoned on. My father was too ill to know what he was doing. I put the papers under his nose, placed a pen in his hand, grabbed an elbow and helped him sign. And they say dishonesty doesn't pay. In our little country town I became an apprentice electronics technician.

Sometimes, the job involved more than just fixing people's black and white TVs. One of my customers was a lovely old chap who had opened the town's first Holden dealership. This was Grandfather Carey. He lived in a flat above the car yard of Carey Motors. While I was busy fixing his TV he would slip me some money and ask me to go down and buy him a bottle of whisky. I suspect he was an alcoholic and the family had cleared all the booze out of his place. Obviously I was under age, but everything was fine. I just told the people in the pub it was for old man Carey. I think his name was Percy; it certainly stated with the letter 'P', as did at least three generations of Careys. Percy's son Paul took over the Holden dealership, but his son Peter was not interested in the cars and utes and station wagons. He horrified everyone by deciding to become a writer.

Peter Carey and I both attended the same primary school: Bacchus Marsh SS28. The 'SS28' told you that it was the twenty-eighth state school built in Victoria. We might have had the same teachers, but that's where any similarities ended. While I was twiddling the knobs of his grandfather's black and white TV and slipping him contraband liquor, Peter went on to become arguably one of Australia's greatest writers winning not one, but two Man Booker prizes for literature.

The unanticipated bonus of my apprenticeship was having to catch a train to Melbourne once a week to attend TAFE at the Royal Melbourne Institute of Technology. Most of the teachers at RMIT were returned soldiers which meant their teaching style was very strict and regimented. Classes were held in the Rex building in Swanston Street. In those days education was not a high priority investment of the government. You weren't allowed to run up or down the stairs in the Rex building because the staircase was about to collapse. Monitors were posted at the top of the stairs to enforce the no-running rule. The place was derelict. Some classrooms had chalk markings on the floors which identified those sections of floorboards which had been condemned. You weren't to walk past the chalk line because you would fall through the floor.

Things were going okay until they introduced the subject of Maths. As I had no idea what they were talking about I failed miserably. A teacher pulled me aside and told me my slide rule calculations were hopeless. "Slide rule?" I asked. He said, "You have no idea what I'm talking about, do you?"
"No."
"When did you leave school, boy?" I recalled that the RMIT enrolment form mentioned that students had to have completed Year 10. I believe I accidentally ticked that box. Before I could answer he said, "You couldn't have done Year 10. That's when you start using a slide rule." Sighing in exasperation he told me to go down to the Co-Op Bookshop and buy a book called *Introduction to the Slide Rule*. It cost me about $1.50. I sat at home and I practised using this thing. The slide rule was really a primitive version of a calculator. The next time around I achieved a credit. There have been so many times like this in my life where my situation could have been quite dire but for those people who went out of their way to help me.

At this stage I was earning about $13 a week and supplemented my meagre income working three nights a week as a garbo. It kept me very fit, but it was a horrible job. There were none of these poofter bins you see today with waste separated and sealed in plastic bags, it was all blood and guts. Dead cats were a special treat.

The local television repair technician who employed me changed my life, but he was not so lucky himself. Later the business went bust. He was convicted of fraud and committed suicide. A pity actually, because he was a good man.

After my Bacchus March employer went broke, the great bureaucracy of the apprenticeship system swung into action and I was offered a job in the Thorne factory in Heidelberg, on the outskirts of Melbourne where I could finish my apprenticeship. If fate had smiled on me in getting me out of the post office, then being taken on at Thorne was like intervention from the Gods. It so happened that a cousin of mine, Albert Hoy, lived not far from Thorne's factory. Although a cousin, he was a generation older than me and became the godfather I never had. Because I was young and enthusiastic I think he saw a reflection of himself in me and took me under his wing. Once, Albert asked me what job I wanted in the factory. "I'd just love to be in the R&D Lab," was my response.

"Right. Who's the guy running the lab?"

"Jim Farmer."

Albert said, "Tell me, does he ever walk through your section of the factory?"

"Yes, every day."

"Okay. What do you say when he says hello?"

"I-I-I say h-h-h-ello." I was incredibly shy.

"Next time he comes through just say, 'Hello, Mr Farmer'".

"Okay."

"Now, he will tell you to call him Jim."

"Right."

"But," advised Albert, "never accept it. Always call him Mr Farmer. That will separate you from the other smart arses." I did exactly as Albert told me and six months later ended up in the R&D Laboratory.

Albert Hoy had the most profound influence on me. He was a descendant of a Chinese family who had come to Australia during the Gold Rush. His father, Joe Hoy, was Chinese, and his mother was my mother's sister. Albert Hoy was a very tall, good-looking man with a long Chinese face. During World War II he worked as a tradesman in an ammunitions factory. Because he was regularly bashed on his way to work they actually cut a gap in the factory's security fence so he could sneak in and out undetected. He spent the five years of the war worrying every night that his house would be burned down. At that time it was politically correct to hate him and bash him: "Asians are Japanese are bad." His experiences inculcated in me a deep and abiding distrust of the notion of political correctness.

Albert was extremely bright and held an executive position with a large electrical manufacturer. When I joined Thorne I latched onto him and he taught me never to accept, but to question, conventional wisdom. On Fridays after work I would find myself at Albert's place and we would talk about what had happened at Thorne during the week. There were not a lot of people for me to talk to and he was my hero. I'd be mouthing off about something and he would say, "Learn to listen." That was one of his core beliefs. To this very day I will find myself in a meeting and hear the voice of my godfather counsel, "Learn to listen." He'd talk of what it was like being Asian and living in Australia. I was fascinated by that. It was from him that I learned that for Asians, silence is a weapon. What was unsaid was just as important as what was said, and that one must not be afraid of silence. Another weapon in the Asian armoury was patience. They have a completely different concept of patience to Westerners. Their approach is 'outwait them, outwait them, always outwait them'. I loved the quasi-military type chats Albert and I often had at his home. When I went into business for myself I was already conditioned to not be xenophobic about Asia. When I was about thirty, his wife called and informed me that he was seriously ill. He was at home and being made comfortable. I spoke to Albert and told him he would always be my hero. Then he died. I was devastated when I heard the news.

I finished my apprenticeship as a television repairman and became an electronics technician. The black and white television was now in its death throes. Gough Whitlam was elected Prime Minister and overnight removed the tariff protection. Any local manufacturer of electronic equipment was doomed. The factory closed, just with a stroke of the pen. A former workmate said to me, "You should get into computers, you know. They are the next big thing." He referred me to an American company he was working for, Digital Equipment Corporation.

I went for an interview and the fact that I'd trained in electronics at quite a reputable technical college and also worked in an R&D lab was a plus. Thorne had one of the few R&D laboratories in the country. This American company had a preference for military-trained recruits, but they'd run out of them. Digital were making mini-computers as opposed to mainframes and the poor bastards were desperate. They were growing at something like forty per cent per annum. After doing a series of IQ and psychological tests the job was mine.

The very first day I was there, my former workmate and friend whispered to me, "Don't forget the scam. Now you've got the job, don't forget the scam." Like almost all American companies, Digital were big on education. They wanted to make a corporate clone out of you and to this end offered three months training in Boston. Each month you were given a test and if you passed they sent you to America. You did three months in Boston and then returned to Melbourne. Also, each year we received a month's holiday. This meant that most employees did their test, went to Boston for three months, and some time down the track took their holidays here at home. The scam was to fail every test every time until the eighth month because you wanted to end up in Boston just when your leave was due, not before. Let me tell you it takes tremendous skill to keep failing an exam. The paper was split into five sections and after falling short of the mark yet again, I would be quizzed on why I had passed section three last month, but failed it this month.

I passed all sections of the exam for the first time in my eighth month. It took the company a month to organise my travel to the United States. Being a loyal employee I suggested they save some money by giving me a round-the-world return ticket. It was cheaper. Head office in America, which paid for the airfare, loved the around-the-world ticket. They were oblivious of the fact that it had taken the local manager eight months to get you over this hurdle. However, the local manager was not that happy. These bright, young smart arses were exploiting the system and he knew it, but he stoically put up with it because it was hard to find people.

For me, this was a life-changing experience. The first time I went to the US, I arrived at Boston's Logan Airport at midnight where a taxi was waiting to take me thirty-five miles to Maynard, Massachusetts, this little hick town. On the way there we ran over a skunk; very smelly, just like the song; a funny experience. Digital were the second biggest computer company on the planet, but no one had heard of them. Public Relations was not their strong suit. It was owned and operated by tech heads. I worked in post-sales, the maintenance area, which boasted a strong cash flow making it about forty-five per cent of the company.

We were always underpaid at Digital, but they were an old-fashioned company with a wonderful American homeliness about it. I know it's fashionable to shit-can Americans, but I always found them very generous people. They were absolutely wonderful to me. Digital epitomised the old school American business culture that I so admired. I was told that if an employee died in the USA, the company didn't give the family lots of money. Instead, the employee's children would receive a university education. It had a real 1950s feel. There were signs on the wall, 'If you enjoy working here, tell a friend, tell a relative'.

Digital were genuinely moral characters. The company folk story went that they sent a field service engineer to do some maintenance work at the New York Stock Exchange. The only problem with this Digital engineer was that he was black and the people who ran the exchange, all white, and some of them possibly racist, threw this negro off the site. For the owners and shareholders of Digital, most, probably all, of whom were white, the NYSE was a must-have client. The incident worked its way up the corporate ladder and eventually landed on the desk of the President of the company. He was white, and a Southern Baptist. Interestingly, there have been more Southern Baptists in the White House than any other religious affiliation. Also, if there is someone who is a self-proclaimed pillar of morality exposed for leading a double life he's odds on to be a Southern Baptist.

The story was that the President of Digital said to the people from the NYSE, "We employed that man. He's qualified to do the job. He stays." The NYSE demanded that Digital take all their equipment out of the stock exchange and never come back. By this time the whole Digital company was in absolute meltdown. The company was risking losing a hugely prestigious client all over one man. And the NYSE cunningly fudged the race issue by then claiming that they threw the guy out because he was incompetent and that Digital's equipment was faulty. The pressure on Digital's President was enormous, but he could not be moved. It was not in his psyche. His tenacity and morality were legendary. He rang the NYSE and told them he had instructed his staff to go down to the exchanges and rip out all their equipment. He called their bluff. The New York Stock Exchange backed down. I actually met the black guy who was at the centre of this controversy. He was a monster of a man, massively taller than me, yet in so many respects just an ordinary guy. I related to and thrived in that type of company culture.

As expected at the end of the three months training in Boston, I had a month's leave owing. What better way to have a holiday than to slip over and tour the UK and Europe before coming home. My round-the-world ticket was business class and I bought a first class Eurail pass. As far as scams go, it was brilliant. It was, of course, the first time I had ever been overseas. I know one is supposed to look at the scenery, but the major observations I remember from that time were the girls. Boston girls look cute, but from the belly button down they are extremely wide. I thought the girls in England looked fantastic until I arrived in Paris. The French are in a class all their own. I'm sure I trekked around museums and that kind of thing and did all the things that one should do. Sometimes, I had to remind myself that only a couple of years before I was pedalling a pushbike around the streets of good old Bacchus Marsh delivering letters.

I arrived back in Australia bursting with enthusiasm. Noticing I had suddenly developed an interest in things elegant and stylish, a friend remarked that I had discovered 'chic'. Much to the horror of my managers I told them I'd decided I didn't like technical things and wanted to work in sales. Against their better judgment they agreed to do this on a trial basis, but that all changed when I brought in the account of the grocery chain G.J. Coles. It was a million dollar contract and one of the largest commercial contracts of its kind in this country. My bosses were very pleased with me.

My manager came into my office one day with a stack of text books. "There you go," he said. "You like reading?"
"I love reading," I replied.
"This one's on marketing, and this book is on management, and this…."
"Thank you, Les, that is really kind. I will read them."
"Well," he said, "you need to read them in the next ten days. We're sending you to Harvard."

The next time I went to Boston they had a helicopter for me. This fellow ran up to me and grabbed my briefcase. Like a fool I tried to fend him off. Turned out he was not a mugger but the pilot and was trying to put my briefcase in the back of the helicopter. One of those glorious moments in my career. The difference between an engineer and a manager in America was a taxi at midnight, or a helicopter during business hours. Each time I flew to the US, I was given a business class ticket. The achievers in America are rewarded. This is not so here in Australia.

I did a two week MBA at Harvard and in those two weeks

I learned more about the world of business than anything I learned along the way in the next thirty years. The lecturers and the people they brought in to talk about the companies they had created were nothing short of brilliant. If I learned nothing else, I discovered the critical importance of cash flow.

At that time I worked for Digital's South Pacific Regional Field Service, or SPRFS. One of the other students told me he worked for Central Europe F.C. There were all these buzz words flying around and I noticed the man next to me appeared to be well into his fifties. At the time I was just under thirty. He seemed a very knowledgeable guy. He was a world traveller, spoke three or four languages and that sort of thing. I wondered why he was on our course, so I said, "Who are you with, Phil?"

"Oh, look," he replied, "the best thing to say is S.P.Y."

Rather than admit I didn't have a clue what that was, I just said, "Oh. Them. S.P.Y."

After that, I started mulling over what it could stand for. South Pacific something? Special Products Yugoslavia? The next morning I happened to be sitting next to Phil and so I said, "Oh, by the way, Phil. Just remind me again. I'm sure I know it, but what is S.P.Y.?"

He looked me in the eye and after a suitably timed pause said, "I'm a spy."

I sat there red-faced for quite some time after that. Phil later told me he specialised in studying data from listening devices which included those that picked up the sounds made by

Russian submarines travelling through the English Channel. The subs left home and traversed the Channel and travelled into the Atlantic sounding like new. About nine weeks later at the end of their voyage they rattled all the way home. From this the Americans knew the Russian subs were very unreliable and it led them to conclude that in the event of a war the Russians' equipment would fall to bits in a few weeks.

The Americans taught me so much. Here's a simple example. In Australia, if an employee has been successful in bringing in a new client, we might reward their achievement by a slap on the back and perhaps shout them a beer one Friday after work. When the Americans give out an award they make sure it is large enough to fit on it the vital information: the name of the person, the date, the details of the achievement such as 'salesperson of the month', and the place. Although you received the award at work in front of your peers, the intended audience for the award was family and friends. Someone visiting the worker's house would notice the award on the mantelpiece, pick it up and know exactly what it was about. This meant the legacy of the award went on long after it had been given. An ever cynical mother-in-law would have to admit that her hapless son-in-law had received an award in recognition of his work.

Life was good to me. I was about twenty-eight. The opportunities available to me were phenomenal. I was doing presentations to the board members of Coles. I had an office, a secretary and a company car. I had married a gorgeous girl, we had a cute little baby boy, and we lived in a three bedroom townhouse in St Kilda. One day I bounced home and announced to Linda, "Great news! I've been promoted to head office. We're moving to Sydney." I was the living, breathing proof that dreams do come true.

Just before our divorce was finalised, Linda said to me, "You know, you never even asked me whether I wanted to move house or anything like that. It absolutely traumatised me. Made me feel worthless." Apparently that offended her. At that time I didn't know why people were so sensitive. When I think about it now, I cringe. It was done out of innocence and enthusiasm. I had no understanding how inconsiderate it was. I had met Linda at work. She worked in logistics and was super cute. In those days you couldn't have a relationship with anyone at work, so one of us had to leave. As I had the better career and was the male, she left. She never forgave me for ruining her career and this was only to make matters worse. By this stage we had a son, James, who was about a year old. As houses in Sydney were three times as expensive as Melbourne properties, we moved from fashionable inner city living at St Kilda to Kellyville in the backblocks of Sydney where there was no public transport, no family or friends, nothing. In the course of developing the suburb they had bulldozed every tree there was and so it was a barren, forlorn, heartless kind of place. It was just terrible. Linda was alone in this miserable place with a little baby.

Whereas I had led a charmed existence in Melbourne, when

we moved to Sydney it all fell to bits. I loved the head office environment. About two thousand people worked for Digital in Sydney. They had one of the towers above the railway line in Chatswood. I was a workaholic and I have to admit that I used to delight in it. Also, I suffered from a yet-to-be diagnosed disease called entrepreneurialism. Still do. Invariably, I took work home with me, which some women find more objectionable than staying back late at the office. Obviously, few relationships can survive that. As well as my marital problems I had a dick-head boss, was passed over for promotion and grumbled to myself about being underpaid. It was the first time I had suffered professional rejection. My poor wife had to go through all the drama of this. I applied for a job with Macroset, a third party maintenance company which had customers like Qantas and HM Customs. They were prepared to pay me double what I was earning at Digital. Then, to my amazement I didn't get the job. I was shattered. I was on the edge. My wife thought I needed therapy. She definitely needed therapy. It was around this time that we learned that our son James was profoundly deaf.

He was born in Melbourne and it wasn't until we came to Sydney that we found this out. We went from doctor to doctor to see what could be done, but essentially they said he was deaf and we should just accept it. This was completely wrong advice. I did the rounds of various specialists and finally found a doctor in Chatswood who put grommets in James's ears and he was fine. Because he hadn't been talking through that critical period he had to have speech therapy at

Macquarie University. Eventually, he worked through all of that and was able to go to a mainstream school.

One day the phone rang. It was the Managing Director of Macroset, Warren Rickard. He said that even though I was unsuccessful in my application for the position of NSW Branch Manager, perhaps I would come in for an interview for the job of National Marketing Manager. I got it, and it was a very good job. I wasn't there long when they were bought out by Bell and Howell. In hindsight it would probably have been wise to stay and work for the new owners. However, I was all over the place emotionally and chose the worst possible time to have an entrepreneurial seizure. I decided to set up my own business, but while that was happening I went and worked for some hare-brained company that brokered second-hand computers.

By this stage I had debts of about $300,000 and climbing, with a veritable army of creditors chasing me. Other than that, I was doing fine. Within days of my arrival, the guy who had hired me remarked to his managerial colleagues, "Isn't that Manly guy something? Since he arrived the phones have done nothing but run hot. He's fantastic." If only he knew the people ringing the place were my creditors.

By now I was desperately struggling and then not one, but two miracles came to pass. I was headhunted by a guy called Mark Gatehouse. We had vaguely known each other at Digital where he held a management position in software. He too had left Digital, had worked for a couple of companies, and was now setting up his own software company and needed someone to sell the software. The other priceless thing that happened was that Mark Gatehouse introduced me to Jennifer McCarthy.

CHAPTER NINE

ELLIOTT ELIAS LURIE

Either accidentally or deliberately, I could never decide which, Lurie adopted a strategy of being a constantly moving target. Every time he appeared in court the case had changed, even if ever so slightly. Originally, he pursued a claim against Julian and me for damages arising out of his 'association' with ITSA. Then an Amended Statement of Claim would appear in which he added additional allegations. While our legal team would be assessing that evidence, Lurie began an appeal against the Magistrate's finding in the laptop case. Just as that was being digested we would receive a Notice of Motion regarding action in the Federal Court over another spurious claim followed soon after by an appeal against the Supreme Court ruling on his fraud conviction. Just as we were coming to grips with that, he would file a supplementary affidavit detailing new evidence in his damages claim. By claiming interest and aggravated damages his demand for $234,256 blew out to a million dollars and beyond. It was like being slowly bitten to death by ducks.

Lurie was a nightmare who dominated our lives. The time wasted at court hearings was nothing compared to his impact behind the scenes. He would ring my office and terrify the receptionists by asking them about the case and then informing them that he was making a note of their comments. An Amended Statement of Claim would be faxed over which would be slightly different from the one posted to our solicitors. You would make the mistake of looking at it and saying to yourself, "I've read that before," and then in court Lurie would argue the variation in the evidence confusing the issue. He muddied the waters brilliantly. There were mentions to attend, hearing days, conferences, affidavits to be prepared, arbitration meetings, responses to particulars to be provided, letters, faxes and phone calls by the hundreds with mountains of documents piling up.

Over the years we learned a little about the murky past of Mr Lurie, but who would know if all or none of it was true. He was born in South Africa in 1955, which made him a good five years younger than me. In 1988 he came to Australia for the first time to set up an office for a South African computer company. He left them soon after and became a self-employed management consultant, operating under the name Halfakey Pty Ltd. Lurie undertook research and development into the standard coding of documents for the tourism industry. This research was independently funded by himself, his father and his uncle and he conducted this privately funded research in the e-commerce field for the next five years. By the time Lurie's family's funds were exhausted in about 1993, his father's and his uncle's houses had been repossessed to recover money which had been borrowed to fund his research.

When Lurie arrived in Australia he carried with him letters of recommendation from some of the world's heavy-weights of industry. There were letters from the Secretariat of the EU, or the South African Standards Association and, of course, companies like Apple and Microsoft. One would see the awesome letterhead and then phrases like: "Thank you for your input," and, "Your ideas deserve serious consideration" would catch your eye and make you believe Lurie had actually been working with them. However, if you examined the letters very closely, which almost no one ever did, what all these august organisations were doing was simply replying to Lurie's letter to them. Obviously, his initial letter was beautifully crafted to elicit a response which made it seem to be a reference from the Gods of Commerce. It was impressive, unless you examined it closely.

Lurie was on unemployment benefits and had been for most of the 1990s. He claimed that he had set up FOI, (Forum of Open Interchange) to assist people in a similar position to himself, that being people with experience in the electronic information industry, temporarily unemployed but eager to find jobs and network. According to Lurie, he and others were being ignored by employers because of their age and the misguided assumption they were not computer savvy. Whether this is truly how Lurie felt, we will never know. I personally believe he was probably angling for government funding as well as to make a quick buck for himself.

I remember once waiting in the lobby for one of the first of our many court appearances. Lurie and I were both sitting on the peeling, leather armchairs opposite each other and trying not to look at one another. Suddenly, this dishevelled, scraggy-looking woman carrying a plastic shopping bag burst into the waiting room and documents went flying everywhere. She made the fatal mistake of standing not far from you-know-who. Lurie immediately slid across and helped her pick up the papers on the floor. Licking his lips he said to her, "I know how you feel. It's not easy being a litigant in person, is it?"

"Good God!" she squealed, "I'm a barrister." She then revealed she was late, had missed her call over and her whole case was now a shambles. It shook me to think some poor soul was paying this mad woman let loose from an asylum a few thousand bucks a day to lose their case for them. However hairbrained she was, she had enough gumption to twig that Lurie was someone to be avoided and cut him dead.

Apart from my divorce, this case with Lurie was really the first time I had been deeply involved in a court case. As I sat there waiting I naively believed that the whole impressive apparatus of the justice system was there for me.

On another occasion, Julian and I arrived at the Federal Court around nine in the morning. When we walked into the building, we bumped into two detectives from the North Sydney Police Station. The police at that station regarded us as absolute legends. They explained that they had been trying to serve four outstanding warrants on Lurie for unpaid fines, totalling thousands of dollars, dating back to 1990. The problem was they couldn't see him anywhere. "Come with us," Julian said. We travelled up to level 18 with the detectives, all as one merry group. The arrangement was that if I saw Lurie I would point him out and keep going so that he couldn't see that we were affiliated with the warrants. Sure enough, as we exited the lift, I spotted Lurie and gave the nod to the coppers. Julian and I then ducked into another courtroom while our erstwhile friend was given his outstanding warrants.

The bailiff called us into court and when Lurie came in he looked noticeably flustered. Never one to pass up an opportunity to kick the opposition when he was down, I turned to him and smiled. "Isn't this the most glorious day? Don't you think?" Nothing but a grumble from Lurie. "You'd have to feel lucky on a day like this."

This hearing only went for about ten minutes before it was adjourned. After yet another wasted day in court Julian and I were packing up to leave when Lurie walked over and said in his condescending, irritating voice, "I think we should have a cup of coffee, chaps."

"Mate, we have no interest in having coffee with you whatsoever," I said as we walked towards the lifts. "You go your way and we'll go ours." The idea of spending any more time with Lurie than we had to was nauseating, but he persisted. "Gentlemen, I think we should have coffee together, now."

This time Julian politely declined as a lift arrived. Neither Julian nor myself wished to be in the same room, let alone the same elevator as Lurie. We suggested that he take this first lift and that we would get the next one. Lurie didn't move, so Julian said, "Okay, we'll get this one, you get the next." Julian and I walked into the lift but Lurie followed us in. He was like that annoying kid at school who did anything to get on your nerves. As we descended to the ground floor, Julian again stated, "We do not wish to have coffee or be with you, Elliott."

As we walked to the Macquarie Street exit Lurie followed. "We are going this way," said Julian, "please, you go the other way. Please leave us alone." When we started walking, he stepped in front of me trying to block my way. He stood very close. Clearly, he didn't need another coffee because I could smell it on his breath. He had his fist clenched in a threatening manner and raised it aggressively. I wasn't the sort of person who ever reacted kindly to threats. "Lurie, you're a crim. And we don't associate with criminals." Instantly, his face blackened in rage. I had hit the mark. As we stepped off he grabbed the collar of my suit and spun me back to face him. I think I did well to remain relatively calm. "Go for it, buddy," I threw back in his face. We eyeballed each other and then he let go my collar and walked off.

Who the hell was Elliott Lurie? Physically, he was easy to forget and hard to remember. I was reminded of the fact that someone once famously described Joseph Stalin as a 'grey blur'. When he became the head of the Communist Party in Russia many of his rivals couldn't put a face to the name. So it was with Lurie. Although the man came to consume thousands of days out of my life, from one hearing to the next I would have trouble remembering who he was.

It wasn't the man's personal features that I remembered, but his suit. Invariably, he appeared in a charcoal grey suit wearing a business shirt and tie. I confess to being not the most observant person and so it was possibly a few years into the case that it struck me one day that it was always the same suit. There was some fraying around the elbow which alerted me to this. Then I realised that it had to be the same shirt. The man owned one suit and one shirt and one wretched tie. That was a revelation.

Julian had heard rumours that he'd once been renowned as a brilliant computer whiz-kid who suffered brain damage and psychological injury as a result of a car accident. We had no idea if this was true or not. He certainly didn't seem stupid or impaired in any way although he was an atrocious speller and his affidavits were riddled with clangers which gave Julian and I some amusement. There are precious few jokes in a courtroom and we clung to whatever amusements we could find. In moments of exasperation, Lurie referred to me as Mr Alan Child (formerly Manly). It was pathetic really, like a Benny Hill joke.

Lurie didn't think or behave like anyone I knew. One day I caught a train to Martin Place and as I was exiting the station who should I spy there at the turnstiles surrounded by a throng of security people but our nefarious friend who had been caught travelling without a ticket. Instinctively, observing Lurie's unruffled composure, I suspected this may have happened before. As I lingered I could hear him telling the officials that he was South African and knew nothing of how the system worked. "I'm just a visitor," he explained. When asked to produce a licence he responded that regrettably he did not possess one. As the railway officials did not have the power of arrest all they could do was issue him with an on-the-spot fine which I suspected, based on my own experiences with Lurie, may have never been paid.

By all accounts Lurie was a devout Catholic, but anti Vatican II and claimed he was being persecuted for his beliefs. Yet in all my considerable dealings with him such views were never aired. The thing that I found hard to get over was the fact that he lived in a boarding house. My experience was that people who lived in boarding houses were invariably middle-aged men who were down on their luck, that being the euphemism for alcoholism, chronic gambling problems, or the last refuge for someone on the run. My family were desperately poor people, I knew lots of poor people, but no one I knew lived in a boarding house. People who are poor often get maligned because they are not sophisticated. However, in my experience poor people are rarely cruel and often incredibly generous. They are the people I relate to more than the well-to-do. But there are the poor and those beyond being poor. When the office of the sheriff attempted a writ of execution at Lurie's boarding house they reported that the debtor was unable to satisfy the debt as he was currently unemployed and owned no goods whatsoever upon which seizure could be effected. Everything in his little room, even the chest of drawers, the little black and white television, the bed and the bed sheets were the property of the landlady. Julian and I sometimes conjectured whether

Lurie had a secret lair somewhere, but somehow I doubt it. I could just picture his solitary suit and shirt hanging off a nail on back of the bedroom door.

Given the intensity of my feelings towards him it was hard for me to discern anything admirable in Lurie. From court documents we knew his date of birth and on those occasions when we were in court on that day, Julian pondered whether to be civil and courteously wish the man a happy birthday. Every now and then the tenacious British Bulldog would disappear and in its place we would have this panting, slobbering, puppy. When Julian was cornered, the bulldog's jaws locked and you were dead for all money; but sometimes he tried to lick the opposition to death. He would tell the court he was glad to be there, or suggest we pass on a birthday wish. To me Lurie was beyond the pale and I could never bring myself to do it. There was even gossip that he had met someone and they had a child together, but I never saw any inkling this might be true.

It was sad, but not in any sentimental sense; just sad in a pathetic way to witness this human being wasting his, and our lives, on this pointless pursuit for nothing. And yet without him, without this half-invisible man, there would have been no floor show at all. It was he who flicked the switch which set the whole cavalcade of the court rolling into town. The courts didn't like Lurie, but he brought them customers. Like the little Dutch boy with his finger in the dyke, all he had to do was extract the digit and this great sea of words swamped all our lives.

ONE ONE FIVE

As we battled it out in court day after day, one was left with the unmistakable feeling that Lurie was playing a losing hand. When he saw this coming he changed tack and suggested that he would be willing to make a deal. "I believe that I will be able to refund all your costs and more," he announced magnanimously to the court, "if ITSA was prepared to become an investor in an exciting new start-up company, Australian Information Management." It so happened that AIM, this brilliant venture, was owned by none other than one Elliott Elias Lurie. In other words, if you give me money, surprise surprise, I'll be able to return your outstanding costs. Our lawyers argued that this was really no deal at all and that if our costs were not paid they would pursue Lurie to the point of bankruptcy. This brought Lurie to his feet. "If you bankrupt me," he warned, "it will escalate the hostility between us to an unprecedented level and lead to an unpredictably long campaign which will have my total focus." I realised at that moment that this was no idle threat. On 4 November 1997, Judge Dillon held that Lurie's causes of action in contract and negligence arising out of the so-called 'joint venture' had failed. Our lawyers were very pleased and to mark the occasion of our win Julian invited me over to his place for a barbeque.

CHAPTER TEN

JULIAN REGINALD DAY

If Julian was Billy Bunter, then I was Ginger Meggs, the red-haired, comic strip larrikin with a healthy disrespect for authority. If a talent for playing snooker is proof of a misspent youth, then reading comics must run a close second. I'm actually old enough to remember reading the Ginger Meggs comic strip.

The thing is, the more I had to do with Julian, the more I wondered if the Billy Bunter jibe was off the mark. There's a term often used in business which describes a person as a 'doorknob'. It's used for people who can facilitate introductions to get you into someone's office. Julian is just such a doorknob. He can get you into the most amazing offices in Sydney. He's a marvellous networker. He's like the six degrees of separation phenomenon personified. If he doesn't know one of the movers and shakers of this city, he knows someone who does. Whenever I attended business functions and it was time to network I would seek refuge in the nearest men's toilet. I am appalling at this. Not Julian. He loves this stuff. He's happy to walk up to a complete stranger and within minutes will have charmed them within an inch of their lives. Like any good politician he has an amazing memory for names. The Information Technology Society of Australia was started after a couple of us chipped in a total of $500. Within ninety days Julian had organised a public debate between IBM and Microsoft at one of the best five star hotels in Australia. All the big names in IT in this country were there. Even more remarkably, Julian has never made any money out of this, I suspect because he likes people a hell of a lot more than he likes money, which probably explains why he never has any.

His expertise in the computer world is project management. He headed up a project for one of the big banks where they saved something like $14 million a month as soon as they switched to Julian's new software system. These bankers went completely off their rockers with excitement, but good old Julian was very deadpan about the whole thing. He loves to play down everything he does. He makes a living by being deadly serious about really exciting projects.

I regarded Julian as a friend, but we rarely socialised. He was friends with everyone except the coin of the realm. He and money have never been friends. If you worked with Julian he would be the guy who borrows $50 to get through to pay day at the end of the fortnight. I don't know what he does with his money. He certainly doesn't. Although I had some savings I lived in a fog when it came to having cash with me when it was most needed. A number of times I have bought a coffee only to discover I am skint. I would be very embarrassed while I waited for one of my staff to come down and pay the ransom.

More than once I silently marvelled at the way Julian had

everything organised when we had to appear in court. He had this great eye for detail and was always well prepared. I had assumed he would, like a lot of IT gurus I dealt with, be a bit all over the place when it came to the crunch. Not so. One day when I remarked on this, he shot back with the famous motto, "Be prepared." He was a scout and proud of it. His passion was the great outdoors. On summer holidays he had worked for his uncle who owned the main boathouse in Henley-on-Thames, Hobbs & Sons, where he scraped down the bottoms of boats, let them out, and took tourists out for a row on that magnificent river. While a boy he joined the scouts where he thrived. I could just picture him in his khaki shorts and peaked hat, sitting around a campfire cooking up a pot of baked beans.

During the time his mother was the Mayor of Henley-on-Thames, she began what became known as the May Fair. When the Queen's Silver Jubilee came around in 1977, Julian came up with the idea of celebrating the event with a competitive raft race on the river. It was a great success, so much so that the local Lions Club has kept it as an annual event.

He told me one of those crazy Julian stories which was so preposterous I just knew it had to be true. After he joined the workforce and was too busy to make a regular commitment to scouting, he thought there must be something he could do for them for a couple of days a year. Out of nowhere Julian came up with this absurd idea of circumnavigating the county of Oxfordshire over a single weekend. It was a considerable distance, perhaps a hundred miles. As rivers formed part of the county boundaries an amphibious craft would be needed, but rather than use something supplied by the army, Julian decided to make his own. Thus Amphinox was born. An engineering firm donated their time to design a craft which comprised two eleven foot aluminium ladders with 44-gallon drums welded on. This was then mounted on a square trolley which had two large dumpy wheels as well as two smaller castors slightly off the ground. He recruited a team of volunteers to push or paddle this amphibious craft along the roads and rivers all the way around the Oxfordshire county boundary in forty-eight hours with the goal of raising money for charity. It sounded like something dreamed up by the producers of Monty Python. Hundreds became involved; they had barricades, road blocks, refreshment stations and police escorts. At the end of the weekend they paddled up the Thames and into the heart of Oxford where their arrival was celebrated as if they'd circumnavigated the globe. For this initiative he was awarded the Chief Commissioner's Commendation for Good Service, the scouting equivalent of an Order of Australia.

He talked fondly of these things and you could just sense that Julian must have missed the eccentricities of old England, and the nostalgic appeal of places like The Old Bell in Henley, a pub, of course, which dates back to 1325.

While Julian was working in the UK, he was assigned a new personal assistant. Her name was Leonie, and she was the first Australian he had ever met. She was doing the continental tour, but her plans fell to pieces once she met Julian. They decided to get married and made plans to have the ceremony in Adelaide. He flew out and met Leonie's family. There were only her mother and her brother, Chris. Her father had died years earlier when he was electrocuted while working for an energy company. Julian's mother and his brother came out for the festivities. After meeting Leonie's family they left them to finalise the wedding arrangements and embarked on a trip up the Sturt Highway into the centre of Australia visiting outback places like Coober Pedy and Alice Springs. For Julian this was a life-changing journey. He found the famous red centre absolutely fascinating and was able to indulge his passion for walking. Julian fell in love with the country and vowed to return. After the wedding they went back to the UK and then emigrated to Sydney in 1986. Leonie found work as a secretary while Julian was in huge demand as a software specialist. She picked up on Julian's interest in scouting and they both became involved in local scouting groups. Sadly, the marriage did not endure and they ended up going their separate ways.

For reasons I have never entirely understood, women were attracted to Julian. This was something I was to see time and again. Even though he had lived in Australia for quite a while there was something unmistakeably English about him. Although he could never be described as handsome, Julian was certainly cuddly in a teddy bear way. The women in my office thought he was a bit of a chick magnet. He pedantically believed the minutes of a committee meeting were as interesting and compelling as anything ever penned by Tolstoy, yet put an ale in his hand and he was transformed. Having divorced Leonie, he told me he was in a long term relationship with someone called Leanne. I think his idea of long-term was a couple of weeks, although I was hardly in a position to be critical of Julian's handling of the fairer sex.

My own divorce saga was the usual thing: recriminations, disputed assets, claims and counterclaims leaving everyone sadder and poorer. My ex-wife went back to New Zealand, had a bloke, as you do, and I used to see our son, James, who was about six-years-old, once a month. Our divorce had a devastating effect on me and was something I never wish to repeat. Despite feeling wary about the opposite sex, when Mark Gatehouse introduced me to Jennifer McCarthy I liked her immediately. She was a well-groomed dark blonde with lumps and bumps in the right places and could talk about any subject, or it would be more accurate to say she enjoyed arguing about every subject. Jennifer was well travelled and had even been to Russia, somewhere I had always wanted to go. I remember she wore beautiful silver and white Art Deco jewellery. I took Jennifer with me to Julian's barbeque.

He had this magnificent unit in a high rise on the water's edge in Drummoyne. There was a great big lawn that took you down to the harbour foreshore. The views over the harbour were spectacular. It was only when we arrived that we realised Julian had a new girlfriend. Julian's latest was Ricki, who had replaced the apparently obsessive-possessive Suzie.

After being introduced to the new girlfriend and knowing Julian, I half-suspected he may not have communicated this new development particularly well to his now ex-girlfriend. Maybe the changing of the guard wasn't expressed clearly and unambiguously. Julian aka Billy Bunter was grilling the sausages and revelling in the role of convivial host. It was one of those unforgettable Sydney afternoons with the sun gleaming on the water as we relaxed in good company with fine wine.

Suddenly, Julian looked up to the sky and remarked, "God, look at that! There goes someone's pants." We all looked up and floating down from the heavens came a pair of trousers, followed soon after by a shirt, and then a singlet or two, then more trousers and shirts. "Oh, the poor bastard," Julian said with a chuckle, "someone's not very popular." And still they sailed down: jackets, socks, shoes and then there was pause in proceedings followed by a lonely pair of underpants which floated into view. "Those are your underpants, darling," Ricki, Julian's new girlfriend exclaimed with horror.

He scampered off and disappeared up however many flights of stairs to get to the bottom of this mystery. Sure enough Julian had neglected to mention to his ex that the relationship was in fact over. She still had a key to the unit and after writing 'Get Fucked' or words to the effect in lipstick over the mirrors in the bathroom she trashed the place. Down below we knew when Julian had arrived at his unit because instead of his clothes coming down, the ex-girlfriend started hurling out the new girlfriend's bras and panties. Snatches of screaming and abuse wafted down from on high. I did half expect at one point that Julian himself might come hurtling over the balcony rail, but figured it would take someone with amazing strength to lift the bugger. Ricki busied herself retrieving their clothes which by now were scattered all over the lawn and at risk of being blown into the harbour. I wasn't sure what the protocol was for guests in situations like this. When in doubt, do nothing. Jennifer and I sat back in our chairs, sipped our wine and admired the boats on the harbour.

CHAPTER ELEVEN

THE STING

Judgment in our case which had started in the twelfth month of 1994 was handed down in the third month of 1998. That's not unusual. Folks frequently wait four years for a decision. Justice Wellington dismissed Lurie's claims and ordered him to pay our costs. When we went back to our barrister's chambers, which were next to the court, her clerk asked, "How did you go?"

"We won!" Fairburn replied jubilantly, "and we won costs. Total annihilation." I couldn't help but empathise with her. I could see how barristers really live on that win. She had fought this great battle and had triumphed. Winning was a great victory, but also being awarded costs made it even sweeter.

I drove home that night feeling exultant as well as relieved. Four years of misery, but not much more than lots of other people have been through. The system worked. Apart from a couple of glitches along the way justice had prevailed. Not only did we win, we won costs. As I drove up the driveway of my home, there, sticking out of the letterbox, was an ominous-looking government gold envelope. Like a clenched fist rising out of a grave. It was from Lurie. He was appealing the findings of Justice Wellington. I was so angry

I could barely control myself.

He then took it to the Supreme Court of NSW. The man could talk, and not just string words together, but bullshit like there was no tomorrow. Why this man didn't pursue a career in the law instead of wasting his time in the IT industry is beyond me. He looked good, he looked smart even in his cheap suit, but no amount of camouflage could completely conceal his contempt for us. In his appeal he claimed that Julian had perjured himself in the statements he had given to the North Sydney Police. The Supreme Court dismissed his appeal and ordered Lurie to pay our costs which were starting to mount up. He told the court that he was suffering from extreme financial hardship and that vexatious litigation from Julian and me was crippling him financially. The judge took no notice and ordered Lurie to pay our $5,000 legal cost estimate as well as $10,000 for counsel.

Revenge, they say, is a dish best served cold. Ross Cameron was my federal member of parliament. I had met him a couple of times and discussed the ubiquitous Mr Lurie. At Cameron's suggestion I wrote him a letter informing him of my suspicion that Lurie was obtaining unemployment benefits illegally. MPs get dozens of letters like this every week. If you write to your local member and complain that the man next door is a drug dealer, what they do is then pen their own letter to the police. "A concerned citizen has written to me and I quote 'they are dealing drugs at 149 Edward Road, Guildford'. I have known the informant to be a reasonable person and a reliable member of the community. I would be grateful if the Commissioner of Police could look into this in due course." In this way the identity of the informant is protected.

Tall, good looking, young and charismatic, Ross Cameron was a rising star in the Liberal Party. As one could imagine his staff were equally young, enthusiastic and ambitious. One of them, known to his colleagues as 'Bingo', was that lethal combination of hot-headed and slap-dash. Bingo saw my letter and should have written to the Department of Social Security passing on the information from an unnamed constituent; instead he sent my entire letter to the DSS. That such a blunder could occur was unfortunate and highly embarrassing; but a second bungle turned my good citizen moment into a complete fiasco. The Department of Social Security, in its wisdom, breached its own protocols and at least a handful of Federal laws and forwarded my full letter on to Mr Lurie confirming a complaint had been made about his claiming benefits to which he was not entitled. As Ross Cameron later remarked, the DSS could only have done this for devilment alone.

When the shit hit the fan, Lurie charged off to Joe Hockey, his local member and a then minister in the Howard Government. In his inimitable style Lurie cherry-picked remarks that Hockey made and from them created a document which purported to summarise their discussions. According to Lurie, Hockey had agreed with him that what was happening was outrageous and a gross miscarriage of justice.

This document was then filed and put before the court as evidence. When that happened all hell broke loose. I managed to get through to Ross Cameron's staff who passed on what was happening to Hockey's people. Hockey was in parliament and had to come out of the house and sort the issue out.

Every week after that Lurie sent out emails to members of parliament complaining about how Cameron was siding with me and that we were doing everything we could to ruin him. It had an impact on Cameron's career and Ross told me he was absolutely driven mad by this incident. Not long after this, Ross Cameron became extremely famous for all the wrong reasons. He was the Liberal Member for Parramatta, one of the most marginal seats in the country and in the middle of a close election campaign admitted to having an extra-marital affair. He was not re-elected. Because of what Cameron went through Lurie's name was well known around the parliament.

Following the setting up of the government's Working Nation program, Lurie had established FOI, the Forum of Open Interchange. It was a cooperative that aimed to promote the interests of its members, specifically in projects concerning the exchange of electronic information. Lurie was the Honorary Secretary as well as the cooperative's Public Officer. However, an ASIC records search revealed that no company was ever registered under the name of FOI, nor for that matter Lurie's other company, Halfakey International.

During this time, coming up to the turn of the century, a subject appeared on the horizon which must have seemed like manna from heaven to IT experts like Lurie. I refer, of course, to the so-called Y2K bug. This was the belief held by computer industry experts that when the year 2000 clicked over, some, perhaps all, the world's computers would, to use the vernacular, shit themselves. Y2K was predicted to cause widespread chaos, international pandemonium, civil unrest and insurrection and possibly pestilence, famine and war. Thousands of tech-heads in the IT industry made an absolute killing out of Y2K. Looking back it must surely be considered one of the greatest, perhaps even the greatest, scam of all time. Pinching an idea from his days with us at ITSA, Lurie started hosting luncheons to promote FOI and one of his favourite debating topics was Y2K. It was the tried and true recipe of good food and wine, convivial company and an entertaining guest speaker.

After some discussion between us, we decided to alert the media about what Lurie was doing. Julian called *A Current Affair* and was put through to one of their researchers. Being au fait with computers, the so-called Y2K bug and Lurie's normal business practices, Julian suggested a 'sting' might be just the thing. Within hours of making the call the researcher, a reporter, two cameramen and a sound recordist arrived on Julian's doorstep and interviewed him.

In October 1998, Elliott Lurie became a television star, but not quite in the way he had ever imagined. Channel Nine's *A Current Affair* covered a story featuring Lurie's FOI business and looked at one of the luncheons they held at Rydges Northside Hotel. On this occasion Lurie himself was the guest speaker, and his topic, the dreaded Y2K bug.

When the network ran promotions for the show, the compere, Mike Munro, highlighted a story about a fraud who kept beating the system. Ever the natural litigant, Lurie sought and obtained an injunction to stop the program going to air. Once this occurred, Mike Munro was beside himself. This was the best thing that had happened in years. New promotions aired in which Munro promised to go on with the fight in the courts and thundered on about the public's right to know the truth. Beneath that mask of gravitas, Munro seemed scarcely able to conceal his glee. All week *A Current Affair* promoted their fight to broadcast the story. In the end Justice David Levine in *Elliott Elias Lurie v The Nine Network* felt that freedom of the press was more important than Lurie's reputation and lifted the injunction. When the show finally went to air it had been heavily promoted in controversial circumstances and the ratings went through the roof. All Lurie managed to do with his injunction was fuel interest in the story.

The cameras showed men in suits arriving and handing over cheques and cash at the luncheon's registry, businessmen networking around the lunch table, and then Lurie standing behind a podium, welcoming everyone to the twelfth FOI luncheon. The guests then enjoyed a gourmet serving of lamb cutlets and salad, accompanied with crisp white wine. Lurie appeared to be quite the host — delicately angling his elbow to refill his guests' glasses. He looked like he could easily get a job as a waiter. All the while, the cameras were filming and Lurie was as proud as punch.

After the end of the formalities of the lunch, reporter Emma Alberici, who later became the ABC's Europe Correspondent, told Lurie that she would love to sit down with him and have a personal one-on-one which, of course, he facilitated. She set him up beautifully. "Congratulations on a successful event today, and thanks so much for having us with you. Now, I understand, Mr Lurie, that you are actually on the dole? Tell me, how is it that you are on the dole and running this business at the same time?"

Lurie just sat there in the pastel patterned chair with his hand on his forehead. Beside him was a fake pot-plant, well no more fake than he was, and behind the chair was a maroon-curtained backdrop. His leg was crossed over his suited pants and his shoes were abnormally polished. He was the proverbial stunned mullet. He could think of nothing to say. "Do you actually want paid employment?" Alberici enquired.
"No, of course not," Lurie replied in his distinctive South African accent. Not his finest hour.

He claimed that it was his social responsibility to provide information to the community and that he made no profit out of such an event. However, Emma Alberici pointed out that this lunch would have brought in probably a thousand dollars.

"Well, our fax distributions alone cost $1,000 a month."
"Mr Lurie," said Alberici, "it does not cost $1,000 to send hundreds of faxes. You can send up to 50,000 faxes via one phone call which costs forty cents." Lurie then reckoned that he put in one hundred and eighty hours per week into the FOI for free. The poor man didn't realise that there are only one hundred and sixty-eight hours in a week. "Well, that doesn't leave a lot of time for you to look for work then, does it?"
"It does if you work on Saturdays and Sundays," Lurie replied.
"Mr Lurie, do you honestly want us to believe, you do all of this for nothing because you want to? Because you are a philanthropist?"
"Yes," he said emphatically, "Because I don't believe in money." This coming from the man who invoiced us for $115.

Here was someone on the dole, running a business with money pouring over the counter defiantly replying, "No, of course not," when asked if he actually wanted paid employment. Incredibly, *A Current Affair* tracked down a very embittered guy who had worked for Lurie, but had never been paid for his services. He described his former employer as a "confidence trickster and scumbag".

A Current Affair also delved into Lurie's family history. It was revealed that he was adopted into a Catholic family in South Africa prior to moving to Australia. They had worked their little hearts out and Elliott had borrowed their savings for a venture that went very south. His relatives had never been repaid their investment despite promises being made.

The Howard Government went into meltdown. It was a sting, of course, and an absolutely brilliant one. It was very topical at the time – dole recipients were costing the taxpayer $28 million a week – and there was pressure on the Howard Government to crack down on social security fraud.

Julian and I had great pleasure in imagining Lurie's face when he first learned Channel Nine wanted to do a story on him. Lurie would have been absolutely beside himself when he put down the phone and would have sat gloating for hours, thinking he was finally recognised by society. This was his big moment. But *A Current Affair* used the Y2K story as their cover to get into Lurie's world.

We went out to celebrate our sting. Julian brought along his girlfriend, Ricki. I liked Ricki, a nice-looking girl, very down-to-earth who hailed from Wollongong. They'd met at Julian's local. She told me she'd had some kind of industrial accident and was going to pick up a small fortune in compensation. Ricki and Julian had dreams of buying a charter boat with the payout and running cruises on the harbour. However, in the end, the boat was not to be. After paying exorbitant legal fees there was only enough left over to buy some new furniture. While it lasted, Ricki was very supportive of Julian and helped him survive this lunatic Lurie.

One day Lurie arrived on their doorstep when Julian wasn't

home. Somehow, he scammed his way through their security system and rapped on their door using the same technique as the police — actually bashing on the door and terrifying anyone on the other side. Poor Ricki was horrified by this thug who then insisted on serving the documents on her. All of which was completely pointless because they had to be served on Julian personally. But this is what Lurie did. It sounds trivial, but the way he went about this caused considerable distress. He traumatised our families.

The sting also revealed that Lurie had received $5,000 in funding from the Commonwealth Bank and was waiting for additional funding of $100,000 from the government. In my capacity as a shareholder of Commonwealth Bank stock, I wrote a poignant letter to them informing them that Lurie had a conviction for fraud and enclosed supporting documentation. CBA responded very smartly and I acquired a magnificent letter from them that they no longer supported Lurie.

As my anonymity had been assured by the Nine Network, I had happily faxed to them the letter so that *A Current Affair* could use it in their segment. But alas, during the show, the top left hand corner of the letter was held close up to the camera and bugger me dead, there was my name and address. You only needed a video player to freeze the image and it was as clear as day. Three days later, another dreaded government gold envelope was sticking out of my mailbox. This time it was a writ for defamation from Lurie.

CHAPTER TWELVE

DEFAMATION

Having failed to get an injunction to stop the story, Lurie then sued Emma Alberici, Mike Munro and the Nine Network seeking damages of $1.3 million for defamation. Unlike Julian and me, Channel Nine had a heavy duty firm of lawyers acting for them, Gilbert and Tobin. Gilbert and Sullivan I called them. Couldn't resist. It was a very brave man indeed who would take on Kerry Packer, the then-owner of the network.

By now I was a courtroom junkie and what better source of amusement could there be than watching someone else face off against Lurie. It also occurred to me that if Channel Nine lost, then we were vindicated: it was not us, but the system which was hopeless. I took a seat in the public gallery and put my feet up on the chairs in front of me. That's the thing I had begun to realise about the courts. To the uninitiated, it's like a place of worship and if one doesn't display suitable solemnity and dignity one may be considered ill-mannered, or, horror of horrors, be found in contempt of court. This is complete rubbish, of course. Do everything you're not supposed to and nothing will happen. Cheer, clap, interject and laugh. Treat them with contempt, treat them like shit and nothing will happen. The courts are run by people terrified of telling anyone to do anything that might offend as they never want to lose a customer. They are all left-wing losers desperate to champion some minority so that they too could be a victim. Political correctness prevents them from functioning as human beings. They are white, they are rich, they have everything to be unhappy about and want to share their misery.

It's only when you start to become part of the system and observe it from the inside that it slowly dawns on you that the whole impressive apparatus of the justice system is there for them, not you. The litigant is a supernumerary, like a spear carrier in a production of *Aida*. The judges, barristers, lawyers, associates, registrars, bailiffs and sheriffs have all been assigned roles commensurate with their status; although there is seating for an audience, most cases play to an empty public gallery. The hapless litigant, the extra with a non-speaking part, provides the plot and funds the production.

One of the solicitors from Gilbert and Sullivan noticed me. He turned around and asked, "Excuse me. Have you got something to do with this case?"
"My name's Manly," I replied, "and I'm the one who tipped Channel Nine off about Lurie."
Something clicked in the solicitor's head. "Ah yes. I've been wanting to talk to you. What do you make of this Lurie chap?"
An idea popped into my head. "Do you remember the kids' cartoon they used to show at the movies, *The Road Runner*"?

"Yeah," the solicitor replied with a puzzled look.
"The Coyote keeps dreaming up all these ways to blow the Road Runner to smithereens, but the plan always backfires and Coyote blows himself up. Lurie's just like the Coyote."
"I'm sorry, are you saying that he'll self-destruct?"
"Yes, but next show he's back. Fucking amazing. It all blows up in his face, but then the Coyote comes up with a new plan, and after that blows up in his face he's back with another bomb, in another episode, courtesy of the sponsors. He loses, but he wins."
By now Channel Nine's barrister was on his feet, poncing around the place. For some reason he reminded me of a big barracuda and so I nicknamed him the Big Barra. He was a big barrel of a man and a rolled gold pompous prick into the bargain. Sitting there close by him looking all innocent was, of course, my weedy little friend, Lurie. I said to Channel Nine's solicitor, "You watch. Lurie will carve your guy up." He dismissed my opinions with a contemptuous gesture and said, "He's a top silk." I knew all about the so-called cream of the Sydney bar. "Yes, I know," I replied, "and he is going to be done like a dinner."

It was an ominous start for the network. Despite all the huffing and puffing and histrionics by Channel Nine's Big Barra, Lurie stitched him up. He couldn't get a grip of this guy. While he argued the finer points of defamation law, Lurie complained the silk was referring to documents that hadn't been filed. They couldn't proceed, much less reach a conclusion, because Lurie said he needed more time and claimed he hadn't been served certain papers. It was like watching a mouse take on an elephant.

During an adjournment the young solicitor from Gilbert and Tobin obviously remembered my earlier warning and sought me out. He dragged the Big Barra behind him and introduced me. "I would like you to meet Alan Manly."
"Oh yes?" said Big Barra, "What do you want?" Despite the humiliation he received at the hands of Lurie, he was like them all, insufferably arrogant.
"I don't want anything," I replied nonchalantly.
Into the breach jumped the solicitor. "I want you two to get together. Mr Manly has been sued for defamation also. Perhaps Mr Manly…"
"Perhaps not," Big Barra interrupted and walked off.

Back we went for more, but it only got worse for Channel Nine. By focusing on very petty procedural issues Lurie was driving them all mad. You're not supposed to enjoy this kind of thing, but I was having the time of my life. To my horror, I found myself a little in awe of my bête noire. The tables had been completely turned. Whereas in almost all defamation actions plaintiffs are terrified of losing to a billion dollar media company and being bankrupted with costs, here Lurie had them over a barrel. He couldn't be bankrupted as he had no assets and all that was happening was that Channel Nine were racking up huge legal costs which would probably dwarf any damages settlement. About fifteen minutes later it was all over. It was Lurie one, Kerry Packer zero. Poor old Big Barra, he was floundering like a beached whale. In the end they made a commercial decision and settled, terms not to be disclosed.

The Channel Nine's story sparked an investigation by Mr Carl Stonehouse from the Department of Social Security into whether Lurie was not unemployed while claiming the social security benefit. On the unemployment forms, Lurie had slapped on "post it" notes listing the names of employers he had approached for work. The "post it" notes were in his handwriting. Everyone Stonehouse contacted either said that Lurie had never applied for the job with them, or had no recollection of ever speaking to him.

The matter went before the AAT (Administrative Appeals Tribunal) which held public hearings and spent a lot of time debating the distinction between a person seeking work as an employee and a person like Lurie, who is essentially self-employed, seeking contract work. Social Security claimed that Lurie was not unemployed and he was not genuinely seeking work within the meaning of the Act. This was supported by Lurie's confession on *A Current Affair* when he said he did not want paid employment. However, the AAT, in its wisdom, found that although Lurie was in fact "unemployed" for the purposes of the Act, there was sufficient evidence that he had satisfied the activity test and had been searching for work. The judgment said that just because he was working and being paid doesn't mean he is employed. Accordingly, the AAT found that Lurie did qualify for Social Security benefits and the decision to put those payments under review was set aside. Lurie was entitled to the dole while he ran his business. Is it any wonder the legal system is such a laughing stock in this country?

CHAPTER THIRTEEN

MARK GATEHOUSE

Mark Gatehouse was a smooth talker. He cottoned on to a software opportunity with a trucking company called Longway. They had a very innovative idea to have a computer system to manage their trucking logistics and employed Gatehouse as a partner. He then headhunted me to sell the QuickSoft system. The company had offices at Flemington Markets. Not the most salubrious address in Sydney, it was located in a very run-down building overlooking the trucking yards and loading docks. Although thousands of tonnes of fruit and vegetables were shipped in and out every day, the markets were surprisingly clean. Unfortunately, the office block at the markets was not subjected to the same rigorous cleaning regime and was a haven for homeless drunks. Every morning I tripped over derros and side-stepped vomit as I made my way up the stairway to the second floor. Hardly the place to be for a man with career aspirations, but there I was.

The workers in the markets were predominantly Italian and they sang like opera singers. Many a time they would burst into song and their voices would resonate beautifully in the enormous sheds. However, their appreciation of the finer things in life was limited. Mark and I were the only people in the entire place who wore suits and the workers would see us and call out, "Here come the poofs again!"

Sometimes I wondered why it was that I often found myself working in these rather desperate places, always under resourced, staggering from cash flow crisis to near catastrophe. It was true that I did have this keen desire to work for myself. The American business writer Michael Gerber calls it an entrepreneurial seizure. I don't know where that came from because I certainly didn't inherit it from my parents. My mother always believed that the very best position in life was a government job. Although it's amazingly easy to start your own business, it's incredibly difficult to stay afloat. Partly for security, partly for strength in numbers, my way into my own business was to form partnerships with other people.

Having benefitted so brilliantly from my creditors ringing me at my previous place of employment, I redirected my creditors to my new office. Again it worked like magic. People were amazed at the number of phone calls I had each day. From memory, I was about $200,000 in the red including about $15,000 owing to American Express. After this nice lady from Amex rang me asking for their $15,000, I said, "Look, I feel totally intimidated. I feel quite ill and I think you're collecting debts with threats."
"Oh no," she wavered.
"Which is illegal," I continued. "Even the way you're speaking now terrifies me."
Like a shot, one of their managers took over the call. He went to great lengths to reassure me that I wasn't being threatened. They just wanted their money back. I reminded him that at no point in time had I denied the debt, nor had

I refused to pay. I was only asking for more time. "Let's talk about what you can do to resolve this before we bankrupt you," he said, ever so politely.

This conversation occurred several years before I became something of an authority on the process of bankruptcy. My response to the man from Amex was that I had really nothing to lose going into bankruptcy, whereas they would lose all their money and no doubt pick up some legal costs along the way. Although my friend pointed out that I was still young and that there were lots of unseen downsides to bankruptcy, I effected an air of casual disregard for the consequences. In the end we cut a deal. I told Amex that I would pay, but only on one condition: that after I paid back the debt with interest I would get to keep my card. I knew that if they took me off their list I'd never get back on. For now it was one less creditor to worry about and I managed to keep my Amex card.

One morning when I was driving to work, I could see lights flashing and hear sirens blaring. As I got closer to the markets I realised the lights and sirens were coming from near our office. I saw Tim, one of the bosses from Longway and asked, "What's happening?"
"You know old Bill, the building manager? His heart," Tim replied.
"Really? He looked so young for a heart attack?"
Tim looked at me. "No, it wasn't a heart attack. A knife in the heart."
"Oh, right," I mumbled.

At that stage Tim had a great big Mercedes; it was a monster of a thing. Longway bought ten new Mercedes trucks and Tim used to boast that they gave him the car for free. It was a beautiful car and he drove it around the markets with great pride. Eventually, some Americans in the trucking industry from Chicago bought him out. The Yanks took over Longway and sent one of their cronies to take control. Their man was straight out of the television program *The Sopranos.* He was an enormous fellow and smoked cigars constantly. I ran into him one day and we started chatting. "How's it all going?" I asked. "Settling in?"

"Oh I love Australia," the Yank replied. "The people are so respectful."

"Respectful?" I queried, thinking to myself, "I get called a poofter every other day."

"Very respectful. When I pull up and park the Mercedes and walk away from it people go over and move their cars so they don't dent mine."

It was only then that I realised that I had parked next to his Mercedes. Others had moved their cars and here was my clapped-out sedan right next to him. He could see what I was thinking and said, "It's fine. Leave it there."

"Really?"

"Really."

Somehow I wasn't so sure, but being sort of semi-paralysed with fear I did nothing. Tim, the original owner of the trucking company, was still floating around at that stage and I told him what had happened. His face clouded over and he said, "You didn't park next to the Mercedes, did you?"

"Well, yeah," I replied.

"You might want to move it. There was a rumour of a contract out on me which is one of the reasons I off-loaded the Mercedes."

"What?"

"Thought I'd better get rid of the car, but the Yank was desperate to have it. You know what they're like; the more I tried to talk him out of it, the more he had to have it. Whoever's driving that car, better look out. Which is kind of a shame, because I loved that car." It was another world.

Mark Gatehouse and I plodded along for a while flogging the QuickSoft system. Gatehouse was a fascinating character. A very gifted guy, software was his speciality. He was a lot of fun, but he was a flawed personality. There were three stages in the life of Gatehouse: eccentric, entertaining and excessive. When I first met him he was at stage one – the eccentric. Broke, but eccentric. He was into mountain bikes. In those days a thousand bucks was a lot of money, but he bought this bloody bike for a thousand dollars. When I broached the obvious question, "How are you going to pay for that bike?" Gatehouse replied honestly, "I don't know." It didn't take him long to come up with a scheme. Every time the delivery day appeared on the calendar, Gatehouse would ring the suppliers and tell them that he wanted some extra options. That way he kept delaying the delivery. They'd tell him it was ready for pick up and then he'd order yet another option. Eventually, he ended up buying the bike, but it was a long, drawn out process.

Gatehouse was charming and easily distracted, especially when it came to women. The guy was a walking disaster and although he was out of control I did owe him for introducing me to Jennifer McCarthy. She was a country girl from Gundagai, NSW. Her parents ran a dry-cleaning store in this town made famous because a hundred or so years ago someone's dog suffered a loss of bowel control on a worker's lunchbox several miles from the town and incredibly this absurd event became immortalised in song putting Gundagai on the map. Jennifer's mother was one of thirteen children. Her father was raised by his siblings. They lived through the Depression and the World War II in dire circumstances: no shoes, ragged clothes, and nary an ounce of fat on any of them. When Jennifer's mother married she only had two children. Incredibly, her grandmother was still having children long after her mother had stopped. It so happened that Jennifer was very bright and education came to her rescue, eventually. Like me, she left school at fifteen and found work in a bank. Then she moved to Canberra where she was employed in a real estate firm before travelling overseas. On her return her boss encouraged her to finish high school, so she was a mature age student in her late twenties when she did that. From there she attended university in Sydney and ended up with a string of degrees. In the space of two generations they went from grinding rural poverty to high academic achievement.

Financially, these were very tough times. I was about $300,000 in debt facing imminent bankruptcy. To make ends meet I rented out the house I owned at Kellyville and lived with Jenny in her apartment. We shared the apartment to help cover the rent, so when my son James came home every fortnight it was a pretty tight squeeze. Certainly, I would never have survived without Jenny's support, and my then-business partner, Mark Gatehouse, was in much the same situation. His wife Sandra kept the money coming in during those lean days. This was not an uncommon situation for the wives of men who had suffered an entrepreneurial seizure.

Although I grew up in a non-intellectual environment, I developed a passion for reading, curiously enough, after I had left school. I read intensively, perhaps as much as twenty hours a week. Although I'd never studied the law for as much as a day I was a prodigious learner and never gave up. My wife complains that I came from the manufacturer without a 'stop' button supplied. With that inexhaustible energy I applied the lessons learned from the school of hard knocks with alacrity. There have been times in my life when I have found myself in trouble, but I am good at getting out of it. I may not have a university degree, but I do have a Masters in Rat Cunning. One of my wife's nicknames for me is 'Ratso'. I take this as being a great compliment, because a rat when cornered can leap a metre. It's very hard to get them to do it. You really have to corner them but when escape seems impossible they can leap a metre. In my life's journey, there have been a few Ratso moments. When an impossible scenario appears on the horizon, Jennifer will come to me and say, "This is a job for Ratso."

Sometimes, in my darker moments, I used to wonder whether it was all worth it. One night Jennifer told me that she believed I had missed my true calling: that I should have been a minister. When she said this I was naturally flattered, because I was always interested in politics and could easily see myself as the Minister for Trade or the Finance Minister. "Oh no," Jennifer wailed, "not that sort of minister. A minister of religion." Imagine that if you can. Certainly, I have the complexion for a man of the cloth who thunders on about fire and brimstone from the pulpit. Whenever I stand to speak in public I change colour from vampire white to manic Irish red. That coupled with a propensity for perspiring like an actor under arc lights makes me appear far more fearsome than I actually am. Also, my mother having been a missionary, I could quote proverbs and scripture verbatim.

I believe Jennifer came to this conclusion after she came with me to an industry function where we were introduced to Peter Costello, who was then the Treasurer and Deputy Prime Minister. Although I had never met Peter Costello before, within minutes of meeting each other we just clicked and you would swear we had known each other all our lives. It's something I can't explain in any logical, rational way. It was true that we both came from Victoria and both had a religious upbringing. Jennifer said later it was amazing to watch: that Costello and I were even physically alike and it was as if I had found my soul-brother.

Personally, I couldn't see any resemblance between me and Costello, but the thing we clearly shared was the fun we had in taking an axe to those pet hobby-horses: political correctness and conventional wisdom. A few days before this function Barry Jones had produced a program for the ALP called 'Knowledge Nation' for which he had produced a huge chart showing all these various tangled lines connecting the numerous components of Australia's education system. When Costello was speaking at our dinner he pulled this chart out from behind the rostrum and with great verve and humour proceeded to tear it to shreds. Cleverly, he tried to explain how it worked, but of course it was impossible to understand. "Should you not follow this," he joked, "and I can see the gentleman over there is not following. Stay with us, sir, stay with us." With the audience in fits of laughter he lampooned the ALP proposal which he dubbed 'Noodle Nation'.

At the time he was the nation's treasurer and we could see his minders at the back of the room trying to wind him up, but when the moment came to leave, there was nowhere for him to go. There were about a hundred people there and obviously the organisers had squeezed in more than could comfortably fit. Costello was completely surrounded by tables packed to the rafters. The signals from the minders were becoming more frantic and Costello tried to squeeze out through the crowd but the throng was jammed solid. Instead he then stood on one of the tables and walked across the tables towards the exit. The audience loved it and started to cheer and clap. With that the treasurer started dancing and shuffled his way over the tables and across the room. He gave us a wave, jumped off the last table, and disappeared. It was an unforgettable performance, as close as politics ever came to vaudeville.

CHAPTER FOURTEEN

SBC

My job was to sell the QuickSoft systems, but I ran around in circles. It was hopeless. The software wasn't flash and the trucking company was burning a lot of money on the project. I spent about a year researching the transport industry and then I invented a very cheap way of tracking parcels. For that breakthrough my story was featured in a national magazine with a picture of me standing next to a Kenworth truck. That was my fifteen minutes of fame. One of my American bosses taught me a valuable lesson. I went into his office one day moaning about a problem that had come up which would mean the end of the world as we know it. He listened very patiently and sympathetically and then quipped, "Thanks for bringing it to my attention. I don't pay you to get into trouble. I only pay you to get out of trouble."

Everything changed when Gatehouse met Dr Bernard Barbier-Buyle, who was the CEO of the Statewide Business College in Sydney. Barbier-Buyle was a short, weedy character with a name which sounded like he was the lead actor in a horror flick. The name, which sounded fictitious, was in fact real, but the man could fake it when he wanted to. At a business conference delegates were startled and impressed to see Barbier-Buyle surrounded by a media scrum as he walked to the podium as one of the keynote speakers. What they didn't know was that he had hired the photographers to make a fuss and enhance his image as a celebrity speaker.

SBC was a very old college and most of the students were girls who wanted to be trained for the legal profession or wanted a shorthand/typing job. The college had this yearning desire to make money out of computers by teaching both girls and boys how to create software programs. Intent on conning our way into looking after the college's computers, Gatehouse and I ended up buying the business. He became the principal of the college and my role was to help him run the place. The idea was to manage the college part time and between the two operations we could hopefully make a living. As any entrepreneur will tell you, two streams of income are better than one.

This was my entry into the college business, such as it was. Initially, I wasn't overly impressed to be there. After all, I had been brought up in a socialist country, Australia, where you couldn't have such a thing as a private university. In most of the world the best schools were private institutions, but here only the government owned universities or TAFE colleges. Private colleges were treated with contempt and disdain.

The deal I had with Gatehouse was that I owned forty per cent of each company and he owned sixty per cent. That was a fair and reasonable deal in a lot of ways. He had used an inheritance to buy SBC for around $50,000 which at the time was more money that I could imagine. It was about half the cost of a Sydney house. However, like many businesses you buy, it probably wasn't worth it. Still, we had to start somewhere and hanging a shingle out and starting from scratch is a lonely, heart-breaking experience. The only people who will tell you that you will do any good are your non-customers. All your friends try to reassure you that there's no way you could possibly fail and then they go home thinking you're mad. "Poor bastard, I feel for his wife," they say. A lot of people say that about me — that they feel for my wife. But what about me?

My role was finding jobs for the students and I used to do this very well. In the end we had about two hundred students. I used to guarantee prospective students jobs at the completion of their courses, which is now illegal, thanks to the usual suspects ripping off some of the students. But because I knew a lot of people in the computer industry, I would ring them up and play cupid and match-make a student with the right company. The skills sets were usually adequate and the students were work ready.

We used to prepare students for the exams which were supervised by the Australian Computer Society. When ACS didn't want to do the exams we were caught a bit flat-footed until we set up ITSA. Because our students were now being accredited through ITSA, I had managed to persuade Gatehouse to underwrite our legal defence against Lurie: Julian and I were being sued as directors and office-holders of ITSA.

During this time I was on the national body of the owners of colleges for international students and it was through this association that I first met Ava Mackay. She was a Eurasian lady who had invested considerable sums of money into a college. Had you told me then that one day Ava and I would be business partners I would never have believed it.

I found my role managing the college and developing its potential very rewarding. In some ways it seemed to me that I had found my niche in life. Dealing with students and academics is never easy, but it is an incredibly stimulating and dynamic environment. Slowly, but inexorably, the business began to prosper and we started making money. When this happened, Gatehouse moved on to stage two: from eccentric to entertaining. The man who not that long ago had bought a bicycle on hire purchase went on a spending spree buying Porsches and lashing out on the latest toys for boys. In his wake, a veritable harem of girlfriends followed. Stage three, the final, God-awful excessive stage, was further down the track.

Meanwhile, Jennifer and I had moved in together. Then, out of the blue, a problem with Linda, my ex-wife, appeared on the horizon. She was in a relationship with a fellow called Scott, who was something like fifteen years older than her. Not long after going back to New Zealand, Linda found a very senior management position in logistics in Canberra and they went to live there. Of course James went with them. Every month my six-year-old son used to come up from Canberra for the weekend and stay. One Sunday night when James was due to go back he said, "I don't want to go back, Daddy. I want to live with you." He was distraught at the thought of going back to Canberra. The six-year-old had had enough. This seemed really odd. I contacted his mother expecting she would have a fit at the thought of losing James. To my amazement she just said, "Okay."

James went back to Canberra and packed two bags: one with clothes, and the other with toys. He told his teacher he was going to live with his Dad and wouldn't be back. All that decision making ability at the age of six and a half. Jennifer and I hired a trailer and went down to Canberra when his step-father was away and brought all his things back. We set about finding him a school.

One of the first things we noticed was that James often woke up in the middle of the night screaming. Then, when getting ready for school he refused to have a shower. It would take ages to try and coax him into the shower. In the end, I had to be in the shower with him. Eventually, James started to feel confident enough to tell us about life in Canberra. Scott, his step-father, terrified him. He made him have cold showers, or locked him in his room as punishment and things like that. Of course, we had no idea any of this had been going on. James came to live with us, but his mother never asked for him back. This was something I could never comprehend. James was the most delightful boy. Linda once told me that she was sometimes asked how she could give up her baby. She replied that she didn't love me, but respected me and trusted me to raise her son.

ONE ONE FIVE

When I received my first Apprehended Violence Order from a policeman, it really hit home what a shit storm I had landed in. We were heading into Christmas when I had this AVO taken out against me. I couldn't go within five hundred metres of Lurie's house — which would have been handy if I had known where he lived. If you have a gun licence you forfeit that and all weapons have to be turned over to the police. It's hard to describe the sickening feeling that drops in your guts when you see a police officer approaching your house with a government gold envelope. What was even worse was when my young son looked up at me in confusion and asked, "What have you done wrong, Daddy? Why is the policeman here?"

I decided to defend myself. The matter was heard in the North Sydney Local Court before Magistrate A. Dalgleish Esq. In his application before the court Lurie complained, "There is litigation in the District and Supreme Courts between myself and a number of defendants including Alan Manly. Mr Manly has a record of abusing and intimidating me. Whenever we meet in court, Alan Manly goads me by calling me a 'crim' and 'scum'. He and Julian Day sit in court mocking and sniggering at my affidavits. At a Federal court hearing Alan Manly repeatedly goaded and taunted me while I was trying to hold a conversation with one of the other defendants. I was very close to striking him for his taunts and vile allegations."

Thankfully, the magistrate was no fool. He was clearly a gay

man and dangerously quick witted. "You mention you have been mocked, Mr Lurie?" the magistrate enquired.
"That's right."
"Whilst I do not in any way endorse mocking," the magistrate explained, "the higher courts suggest that mocking is possibly even healthy in a democracy. Australians characteristically haven't taken themselves too seriously, so many a person listening to an Australian might find mocking is sometimes almost a greeting. Close friends have been known to say to one another, 'How are you, you old bastard,' for example."

AVOs were originally intended to protect women from being bashed by their husbands. Because of this, the standard AVO form has this question: "Are you fearful that the person will move back in with you?" The person being, of course, the ogre husband. Well, when Lurie filled in the AVO form he ticked all the boxes "Yes", obviously without really reading the questions.

The magistrate had woken up by now to the fact that this whole thing was a farce and so he asked Lurie this same question: "Are you fearful that the person will move back in with you?" Having forgotten he had ticked this question Lurie looked all at sea and didn't know what to say. Enjoying his discomfort, the magistrate turned to me and with a smile asked, "Well, Mr Manly, for the record is there any possibility of you moving back in?"
"I would sooner die."
"I assume that is a no. Mr Lurie, has Mr Manly ever lived

with you in the past?"
"Well, no." Lurie conceded.
"Has he ever asked to live with you?"
"No."
"Then why are you seeking an AVO and using this as one of your arguments?" Before he could say anything the magistrate went on, "Do you fear violence? Or, do you fear for your life?" There was a pause which I guess said it all. Magistrate Dalgleish then rounded on Lurie and absolutely castigated him for wasting the court's time with an application for a serious order which appeared to have no basis in fact. Lurie's application for an AVO was rejected. He packed up all his files and stormed out of the courtroom, pushing past people in an aggressive manner. Unbeknown to me, Lurie went to the front desk, took the original application and used white-out to change fourteen words and resubmitted an application for a second AVO. They stamped it and he was back in business.

Going home after a day in court became a nightmare. I swear by the time I arrived at the house, Lurie would have another government gold envelope waiting in my letterbox. There was by this time an endless bombardment of documents arriving at my place. How do you respond to this? I tried talking about it and I even tried writing about it. The problem with talking is that you bore people witless. The problem with writing was that when I did that I found I couldn't do it without starting to cry. It absolutely traumatised me. I knew I had to be obsessed to survive and became obsessed with surviving. Until the day Lurie appeared in our lives I had been doing fine. The impact of that unrelenting battle robbed me of some of the best years of my life.

I think what assisted our survival as a couple was that Jennifer very wisely kept herself apart from it all. She wouldn't let herself drown in this shit and because of that our home was a place of refuge and sanity. So often you see couples who become joined at the hip when embroiled in legal action and it seems to fester a feeding frenzy which in turn destroys them. The downside for me was the intense loneliness I experienced. My wife switched off, my son didn't understand, and I wasn't game to tell them how bad it was.

Like any obsessed person I could talk for hours about my Lurie gloom. I could clear the house talking about my problems. Someone who did cop an earful was my older brother, David. By this time he had risen through the ranks and was now an Inspector of Police in Victoria. He listened and provided wise counsel. I particularly remember one conversation where I was complaining that these court cases were spiralling out of control. "It sounds to me," David said gravely, "like the guy's a blackmailer."

"Really?"

"Instead of having compromising photos of you doing something you shouldn't, he's holding your life for ransom."

"No, I can't agree," I replied. "I don't think this is anything like that."

My brother ignored me. "You have to be very careful, Alan."

"Do you think he's violent?" I asked.

"No, not him. You. I'm not worried about him. Blackmailers usually die in the most violent and savage way. If we find a body that's been stabbed twenty times, the first thing we look for is extortion. You can't pay them out. Even if you give them money they will always come back and come back and come back. More often than not they meet their end from an enraged person who has nothing left to lose and are stabbed to death in a frenzy. Now with you, with your temperament, you need to be very careful."

"Is that so?" I said.

My brother continued, "I really worry about that. Don't get too close to him because you just may snap and kill the mongrel."

The second AVO was struck out as being frivolous and vexatious. Even though these were victories against a sworn enemy, nothing could compensate for the humiliation of having a police car pull up outside your house and a cop walk across your front lawn in full view of your neighbours and hand deliver a court order against you.

CHAPTER FIFTEEN

THE COLLEGE OF HARD KNOCKS

By this stage Mark Gatehouse had become different from the guy I first met. He was a very gifted man in terms of computer software and that was where his passion lay. Whereas I had been the one building up the college and was thoroughly enjoying it, Mark could never get a fix on it. I had really twigged onto a concept of exporting education. Within nine months of taking over the college I made my first trip to China. This was not long after Tiananmen Square. There are always great opportunities when no other fool is game to go there. The Chinese loved this. It showed we had confidence in them and because of the lockdowns in force we were able to see many more government officials than we had ever anticipated.

There were virtually no white businessmen there at all. This was very much the old China, before Deng Xing Peng had really loosened the place up. The only way in was with Air China, 'CAAC', via Hong Kong. The aptly named 'CAAC' was the airline of last resort. One look at the crew and you knew they were not relying on charm to keep you on board. The hostesses brought out our in-flight meal in these old polystyrene containers that looked like, and probably were, ex-McDonald burger containers. You'd have to conclude it was actually tossed salad because she actually threw them at the passengers. The Chinese were not used to seeing visitors from other countries. To them the epitome of the 'foreign devil', or 'gwailo', was someone with red hair and green eyes. It so happened I was blessed with both. On the plane children would stop, stare and point; adults would vacate seats beside me.

Landing in Beijing was an experience I never thought I'd survive. It was at the old airport. It was totally rural. I swear I saw a guy on a pushbike crossing the runway as we were about to land. The engines screamed, smoke poured out from the tyres, and the plane taxied for ever and ever. I went from thinking this must be the longest runway in the world to wondering if the plane was going to stop. I thought to myself, "Fuck me dead. This is the end!" Eventually, the plane slowed and taxied to the terminal which was absolutely prehistoric. Not a computer screen anywhere. It was all paper based.

Although our college didn't have any Chinese students at that stage, one of the big colleges in Sydney with a lot of Chinese students had collapsed under a mountain of debt. I took with me a young Chinese businessman who I'd met in Sydney. His name was Lee Rong and I made him an agent of the college, something which Mark Gatehouse was not keen on at all. Lee Rong got me in to see government officials, managed to arrange an interview with me on Chinese television and organised invitations for Jennifer and me to attend a banquet as guests of honour in the Great Hall of the People. Lee Rong's father babysat our son. We gave our son three bits of paper on which were written in Chinese: "I want a drink", "I want food" and "I want to go to the toilet." Later we found out the father could read English. We also discovered later that the father didn't babysit our son. A cousin was brought in to do it. It's like one of those shadow puppet plays - there's the puppet and then the shadow: two stories. It was very Asian that the father would babysit. The shadow story was that the cousin looked after him, but the father received full credit. We thanked the father profusely and this became our bond with the family. From my experience with Asian culture, children acquire 'uncles' and 'aunts' through friendship. Lee Rong was an 'uncle' of James and therefore his father was obliged to look after him.

Lee Rong was very successful as an agent and found a thousand students for us. Within a relatively short period of time Lee Rong became famous as the biggest agent in China. He is now the biggest education agent in the world. The ultimate goal in China is to become famous. They don't want to just be rich, because being famous means you are rich; you have everything. We say 'fame and fortune', they just say 'fame'. Our enrolments went from two hundred to fifteen hundred and business was booming.

I was now responsible for the day-to-day running of the college. Because of our growth we seemed to be chronically under-staffed. We needed an 'academic' for Business Studies and a man called Charles Claymore responded to our advertisement. At that time Charles would have been about fifty, but he looked sixty-five. He was the same height as me, five foot eleven, skinny, and with a lined, craggy face. He breezed into our lives as a teacher. He was highly qualified and quite capable, and had run colleges before. Because of his experience, Claymore was soon in a management position in the college.

There's a suburb of Sydney called Claymore. It used to be his family's estate. He told me a tale of being recently divorced and his company being bought out as part of the property settlement. People may remember that years back there was a pizza home-delivery company which had as a marketing gimmick a huge telephone hand-piece on the top of a car. That was Claymore. He was quite an entrepreneurial character. The phone on the car didn't work, of course — it just reinforced the whole idea that you rang for your pizza. Claymore introduced the concept of mass-produced pizzas. There was no shopfront. It was a very clever business model and it was bought out by Pizza Hut, whose owners were Pepsi. Claymore worked for them for a period of time and was very successful until disaster struck. He told me this bizarre story that he answered the phone at Pepsi during a thunderstorm. Lightning hit the phone and went straight through that and into his shoulder. Later, he had to have his shoulder rebuilt, but thereafter suffered from intense and chronic shoulder pain.

One summer evening at about seven o'clock at the college, I went down to the carpark where I happened to notice a girl hanging around. I say girl because she was about twenty-one, but could have passed for a fifteen-year-old. The Chalmers Street carpark had to be the grottiest one in town. Why would a beautiful young woman be hanging around there? Everyone had gone home and there were only two cars left: Claymore's and mine. I knew she wasn't waiting for me. Stupidly, I asked, "Can I help you?" Sometimes, overseas students do get lost.

"Oh no, please. I waiting Charles," she replied in passable English.

She was as slender as a champagne flute and just as lethal. I looked at her and thought, "Isn't that a stroke of luck? There you are in that semi-translucent dress on a summer's evening waiting for our new principal."

This was the first time I had clapped eyes on Christina, but I had heard of her before. One of our teachers had reported an incident where Christina arrived late for class. She walked in bold as brass, sat on the lap of one of the students and began kissing him passionately. Unwisely, the teacher decided to ignore this assuming Christina would then take her seat. No such luck. Christina turned it on and by all accounts was doing everything but having sex right there in the classroom.

Within the blink of an eye she was working in the office. Charles put her in charge of something. Christina claimed to be from Mexico, but was apparently Bolivian and out here on a student visa. She was a very good-looking girl with a gorgeous body invariably dressed in a translucent dress which made her G-string very visible. It was just a sex-tease show. I thought to myself, "We are fucked. The second-in-charge of the college is having an affair with one of the students." She twirled her hair and walked the corridors like a model on a fashion show runway. Never before had I seen sex used as a weapon like this. Even her Spanish accent — fake or real, who could tell — seemed a tease. Men in the college were totally distracted. One day, Jennifer had the temerity to ask Christina if she had something more corporate to wear. Christina, whose beautiful breasts were falling out of her bra, replied, "I am wanting to be, how you say, serious; but Charles he tell me, 'You wear this to office.' " Need I remind the reader that I was in charge of this fiasco.

One day when we were discussing the college business and I alluded to some tensions between Mark Gatehouse and myself, Charles said to me, "Why don't you buy Gatehouse out?"

"With what?" I responded. "I don't have any money."

Ignoring my remarks Claymore added, "I reckon you could buy Gatehouse out for a bit under a million."

Assuming he was daydreaming out aloud I agreed, "That would be about right."

"You know," Claymore said quite matter-of-factly, "I've got a million bucks in the bank." As this was coming from one of my staff who drove a clapped-out white van that the average painter wouldn't be seen dead in, I was momentarily speechless.

The thing about Claymore was that he was forever pulling rabbits out of the hat. The next day he walked into my office and handed me an ANZ bank account statement. It confirmed he had over a million dollars in his account. In those days a million bucks was an awful lot of money. You could buy a very plush house in Sydney with harbour views for just half that. A plan was developed where Claymore and I would own the college jointly and buy Gatehouse out. Because I was still in a business partnership with Gatehouse, Claymore and I agreed that it would be simpler if I remained out of the picture for the time being. In the end, Claymore made a cash offer to Gatehouse to buy the college for $930,000. Then it all started to unravel. Claymore was supposed to register a company, but made a 'mistake' with the documentation which enabled Gatehouse to do a search and conclude the vehicle being used to buy him out had me listed as a director. I later learned this 'error' worked to Charles Claymore's advantage. My relationship with Gatehouse was now breached and he accused me of underhanded treachery.

While all this was happening, Claymore and his Mexican/ Bolivian girlfriend, Christina, started living together. He must have thought he was superman. Here he was a fifty-something man with a twenty-something girlfriend, a great job, and a million in cash in the bank.

Mark Gatehouse then made the dreadful mistake of assuming that if we were offering to pay him about million dollars, then the college must be worth ten times as much. This is the strategy that a virgin uses until she's an old maid, isn't it? You do have to cash in the chips sometime, honey. In retrospect, our offer was way over the top, but not from Mark Gatehouse's perspective. After a lot of argy-bargy I got all the little ducks in a line. A price was arrived at and the deal done.

On the morning of the day of settlement I woke up feeling tired after a sleepless night. The man who was going to write a cheque that day for $930,000 was Claymore. I thought I should touch base with Claymore, gee him up if he needed it, just make sure everything was okay. At about seven thirty, I rang Charles at home, but the phone was engaged. I kept dialling yet it was constantly engaged. Things were really on the line with Gatehouse and I remember thinking to myself, "Shit, this isn't the day for something to go wrong." Before phones went digital there was this odd thing which could happen on the analogue system where if you rang someone at the exact moment they picked up their phone to make a call you went straight through to them. It didn't ring or anything; you dialled and suddenly you could talk to the person you had called. This is exactly what happened on this particular morning. I rang Charles's number again, but before it even rang, Christina said, "Hello?" When she realised it was me she said, "Oh, I was just about to dial you."

"I've been trying to ring," I explained, "but the phone has been busy."

"I was using the telephone," she replied. "Charles is asleep. I no can wake him."

"Do you mean he's sleeping, or he's unconscious?"

"Yes, unconscious."

My wife called an ambulance and then I raced over to his

place in Alexandria. Christina let me in. Immediately, I was struck by the fact that he lived in such a tiny, horrible flat. Claymore was unconscious on the bed and the thing that I can never forget was that he had his underpants on. He had a pulse, but that was about it. I couldn't revive him and even tried throwing cold water on him. I started doing CPR until the ambulance arrived. They took over and rushed him to hospital. As we drove to the hospital two things kept churning over in my mind. Who the hell had she been on the phone to? Certainly not the ambulance. We were the ones who called them. And, I wondered, why would a man with this hot young girlfriend be sleeping in his underpants? Very few men sleep in underpants. I thought that was weird.

At the hospital we waited out in the public area with Christina who was wearing her usual translucent clothing. The doctors were ogling her while Christina insisted in her sexy accent that she was Charles's fiancée. As he was clearly at least twice her age they assumed she was just some floozy, or worse, and wouldn't take her seriously. I inherited the position of friend and they spoke directly to me. The situation was extremely grave. There was a chance that he might be brain dead. Into my head popped this memory of Claymore telling me that he was in remission from some form of cancer. When I mentioned this the doctors were incredulous. After testing for this they said there was no trace of cancer whatsoever. Charles had taken an overdose of something and they desperately needed to know what he had taken. We asked Christina, but she claimed she knew nothing about an overdose. They told us that it was better that we find what it was, rather than for them to try and second-guess which drug it was. In the end, I was asked to go back to the apartment and find what he had taken.

We took off back to Claymore's place. I went through the bedroom searching for either a suicide note, or drugs of some sort, and what hit me was that there was not a single pharmaceutical in the entire apartment. Amazing. Not even an aspirin. I tipped out all the drawers, went through the rubbish bins and tore the place apart. The guy had a million things wrong with him and was on all sorts of medication, but there was nary a pill to be found. The more I thought about it the more I believed that Christina had never intended calling me or calling an ambulance. She'd also managed to hide any incriminating drugs before I arrived. Back at the hospital they couldn't believe my story and I could see that they were thinking I was covering something up.

Jennifer left to let the solicitors know what was happening and to delay settlement whilst I maintained a bedside vigil with the fiancée. Charles was hooked up to machines with tubes all over the place, still unconscious, still gravely ill. At a moment when we were alone Christina caught my eye and said, "I know how to do Charles's signature."
"What?"
"If he dies you won't own the college. I could sign the cheque." An unforgettable moment. On the other side of the bed she wriggled slightly in her chair and there was suddenly more cleavage on show and the skirt hitched a notch higher than before. Her eyes locked on to mine like heat-

seeking missiles and she started twirling her hair with abandon. "Forging someone's signature," I heard myself saying, "is a criminal offence."

To the surprise of the doctors — and everyone else — Charles pulled through and made a full recovery. Claymore's story was that after being struck by lightning he had constant shoulder pain and was given morphine for pain management. Somehow, he had miscalculated and accidentally overdosed. As there hadn't been any sign of any drugs in the house I didn't believe this cock-and-bull story for a single minute. The ambos gave me credit for saving his life, but I believe that only happened because I rang his home that morning at the precise moment that Christina picked up the phone. One of the girls in the office at work mentioned that she had overheard Christina on the phone consulting with Chinese herbalists because Claymore was impotent. It had reached the stage with Charles that you never really knew what was true and what wasn't.

At least my business partner was alive, but while he was recuperating he confessed that the million dollars had disappeared from his bank account. According to Claymore some opportunity overseas too good to be true came up and the money was gone. I decided to say nothing about my bedside conversation with Christina. I joined the dots and concluded that Claymore's 'accidental overdose' had something to do with the missing million, but his condition was fragile and I couldn't go there. The whole thing was becoming murkier by the moment. We'd made an offer of close to one million dollars to buy the company, but now had no money to complete the sale. Now I was well and truly fucked. Ratso was getting pushed into a corner. I'd been left high and dry with no funding and an antagonistic sixty per cent shareholder in Mark Gatehouse. We had put this deal to Gatehouse, who was no fool, but he wasn't always as commercially savvy as he thought and his life was spiralling out of control. The staff at the software business were more harem than workforce and the constant catfights among his various girlfriends were distracting him. What was left of our 'partnership' was eroding fast. Things were going wrong so quickly I was really starting to wonder if I would get through it.

"The good news," said Claymore, "is that I know a guy in Singapore who will give us the money." Charles and I flew to Singapore to raise finance from the usual ubiquitous rich Chinese guys. I was in my hotel room when the phone rang. It was Charles. "I really need you to do me a favour."

"Like what?" I asked.

"I am in pain. Could you just come to my room and I will explain all."

By the time I walked into his room he was in a foetal position on the bed. I have no idea how I got into his room, but I was shocked at what I saw. "I need morphine, desperately," he whimpered. "I am in pain."

"Are you kidding?" I replied. "Here, in Singapore. Morphine?" Charles lay on the bed moaning. I picked up the phone and rang the concierge. "Do you happen to know where I can get some morphine?" I enquired as matter-of-

factly as I could. "My business partner is in a lot of pain from…" I looked over at Charles. "From…?"
"Cancer," he said.
"From cancer," I repeated.
The concierge answered, "You need a doctor."

Some time later a doctor arrived accompanied by someone who he had obviously brought along as a witness. He wanted to know what we were doing in Singapore. "A business meeting," I explained. The doctor examined Claymore and satisfied that he was in pain, gave him a shot. Within minutes Claymore was up off the bed, happy as could be. This was my first real up-close experience of drugs. The doctor was very cautious – only accepted payment in local currency and issued a receipt. I was then handed a syringe and some drugs by the doctor who said, "In four hours you'll have to give it to him again, and again in the morning."
"Okay," I replied.
"Mate," Claymore butted in, "not everyone can do this. You've got to put the syringe deep into the muscle," demonstrating the action for my benefit.

Several hours later it was time for Claymore to have another shot. I picked up the syringe. I was surprised at just how big it was. It was a serious man's syringe. "Right, put it in hard," Claymore instructed. "Just be brave and put it in as hard as you can." Obviously, he could not see the malevolent fury on my face. Wham! Taking my frustrations out on him I jammed the syringe in with such force the poor bastard screamed in pain. "I think you've hit the bone," he wailed. He was lucky. I was so angry with him I could have shot the prick.

Singapore was a wild goose chase. We didn't get the money. Claymore disgusted me. I realised he was addicted to morphine and had my doubts about him having cancer. He was a bit of a Walter Mitty character.

Incredibly, in the middle of all, this Claymore announced that he and Christina were getting married and asked me to be the best man. I was too stunned to decline. It turned out to be the wedding from hell. The ceremony was held at the Novotel, Brighton le Sands. Minutes before the ceremony the child bride and groom were screaming at each other in the foyer. Because of the poor acoustics of the place the guests heard every word of that God-awful row. Then she refused to come out of the toilet. We all waited patiently, and then peace reigned among us, she dried up her tears and the ceremony resumed.

As I was standing there next to Claymore his bride walked up the aisle looking resplendent. Claymore's son from his first marriage, who was about thirty, looked at the bride and exclaimed in a low whisper that everyone heard, "There goes a million dollars." Claymore was so blinded by Christina he assumed his son meant she looked like a million dollars and threw his son a smile. Being the mercenary bastard that I am, I suspected his son was bemoaning the loss of his inheritance and could not help but admire his son's reasonably accurate valuation of the business. Charles insisted that there be no speeches whatsoever, which had the knock-on effect of making people think that it might be rude to talk too much. Although a few chatted quietly among themselves there was this eerie, soulless silence and no one seemed to know whether they were allowed to start eating, or start talking, or do anything. As the guests were looking uncomfortable I was then instructed to make an announcement. Feeling like a complete idiot, I rose to my feet and said, "Charles said to please start eating now."

As the meal progressed the bride became unwell. She left the table, went out through the beautiful French doors and on to the balcony from where we could hear the unmistakable sounds of her vomiting. We, the guests, endeavoured to enjoy our splendid dinner to the unforgettable melody of the bride throwing up in full technicolour. No one said a word which, of course, only made it worse as there was this deadly silence apart from the sound of that girl heaving her heart out. The bride returned, as unobtrusively as it is possible for a bride to be at her own wedding. A murmur went through the bridal table. A maid was called for. A few minutes later an Eastern European woman of enormous proportions appeared carrying a bucket, and with all the delicacy of cement truck driver she waddled straight past the bridal table, opened the French doors and with a great swoosh hurled the bucket of sand on to the vomit. It was a hard act to follow.

One of the guests said to me, "What do you think of Christina?"

"Well, she's certainly a good-looking chick," I replied. "She's the type that you'd like to borrow for the weekend, but you'd certainly give her back on the Monday." I think I became famous for that quote, although people misjudge me at times. Christina was cute in her own way. Our little bedside chat vis-à-vis the forging of a cheque for a million bucks was something I never spoke about to another soul. There was no point telling Claymore — he would never have believed me. At least Claymore looked happy and just as well. He was not long for this world.

After the wedding, Charles went behind my back and tried to cut a deal with Gatehouse. When he did that Gatehouse tried to cut everyone out of the action and take complete control of the college. While this nest of vipers were tearing each other's eyes out, I was managing the business and dealing with Lurie on an almost daily basis.

It very quickly became lawyers at fifty paces. The main legal argument was that there were two businesses and two partners. One business was the computer company which was significantly run by one partner, Gatehouse, who was there every day. The other was the college business which was significantly run by the other partner, me, who was also there every day. Whilst I only had forty per cent of the college business I had probably contributed to at least fifty per cent of its value. However, I had limited financial resources and could not match Gatehouse's legal firepower.

My solicitor and I went through six years of work diaries

and produced a forty-page affidavit which painted a crystal-clear picture of my involvement in the college and the significant contribution I had made to its development. When I wheeled into court a trolley with all my diaries on it Gatehouse's very expensive barrister immediately turned to him and said, "We're fucked."

After hearing some of the initial argument, the judge left the court and later returned accompanied by a posse of sheriffs. "Okay," asked the judge, "everyone here?" He then turned to the sheriffs and said, "Lock the doors." It was a lock-up. According to the judge this dispute over the college could have immediate impact on several thousand Asian students who were in this country on student visas. He saw it as a matter of urgent public concern and announced, "Ladies and gentlemen, no one will be leaving this courtroom until this matter is resolved." Down went the gavel. My solicitor whispered to me, "Get phone batteries and sandwiches — fast."

In the lead up to the court case Gatehouse made life as difficult as possible for me. He referred to the sale as a "court-ordered settlement" which I felt put my departure in a bad light. This made me quite unemployable in the industry. Because of this I pushed for a payout and Gatehouse could have the college all to himself. Our lawyers argued, tempers flared, but by about two in the morning we had reached an agreement. The Statewide Business College went to Mark Gatehouse and I received a couple of hundred thousand dollars. There was a non-compete clause and I could not work in the private education industry for three years. Although the money seemed like a windfall, this was a complete disaster for me. Legal fees took a sizeable chunk. I was unemployed and from now on Julian and I would have to foot the legal bills if we were to win the fight against Lurie.

CHAPTER SIXTEEN

BANKRUPT THE BASTARD

It was around this time that the idea to bankrupt Lurie surfaced. Our barrister at the time, Karen Fairburn, advised us that once we made the villain bankrupt he would not be able to hound us anymore and it would really be the end. "The indisputable fact," Fairburn announced, "is that a bankrupt cannot commence legal action." Those words became like a mantra for me: a bankrupt cannot commence legal action. The other indisputable fact was that Lurie had been ordered by the courts to pay our costs. He owed us money. Naturally, I was too polite to ask why all this hadn't been suggested earlier. It also occurred to me that at this point in time my own financial situation was dire, but hopefully not terminal. As Karen was a bankruptcy partner in the practice she would act on our behalf.

Our solicitor, Greg Donnelly, aka 'Fatso', happened to be Fairburn's ex-husband. It was he who politely pointed out that Karen was relatively new to the bankruptcy area. Donnelly then wrote a letter to Julian and me which was absolutely profound. He suggested that if we were going to go for costs and then proceed to bankrupt Lurie, we should do it ourselves. It was an astonishing letter from a solicitor. Donnelly pointed out that this was an incredibly difficult, long and arduous process, but that we could and should do it on our own.

The thing is when you win costs, you don't actually get back all your costs. If a judge awards you costs then the legal fees which you racked up have to be 'taxed', that is, they have to be itemised and scrutinised by a barrister and calculated in accordance with the *Legal Professions Act.* It's like the Medicare trick where you get back about eighty-five per cent of your doctor's bill. A costs assessor, Mr Simon Blackwood, was appointed by the court to tax our legal fees.

He sent me a letter and so I rang him up and said, "I received your letter." Blackwood then berated me for having the temerity to ring him. "Well, with all due respect," I explained, sounding more and more like a lawyer every day, "you wrote to me and it says here at the bottom of your letter: 'please contact me if you require further information'. So I am following your instructions." He had no come back to that.

"Well," stammered Blackwood, "you had better get your barrister's diary. I need to see how every minute has been duly charged." When I rang Fairburn she went into a spin. "Diary?" she moaned, "I think I've lost my diary." The dog had eaten her homework. Detecting cynicism in my voice she pointed out that she had spent far more hours on the case than she ever actually charged for. "We just charge what we think the client can afford, but it is always less than the hours we do." At that point she confessed that she had also worked on a Sunday. All I cared about at this point was that we have the evidence Blackwood needed to tax the costs. In the end, Fairburn miraculously found her diary and we had the information we needed.

Towards the end of this taxing business I think Blackwood actually sympathised with me. I suppose compared to Lurie I was quite normal. He assessed our taxed costs to be $35,808.44.

Our solicitor, Greg Donnelly, also emphasised in his letter the critical importance of Julian and me personally serving documents on Lurie. This would help to make our bankruptcy case watertight. To make a person bankrupt, you first have to serve them a bankruptcy notice in person. Becoming a bankrupt is actually a loss of their liberty: their liberty to trade. So we had to serve Lurie personally.

As we had anticipated it took a lot of work just to find him. We hired a private investigation firm. They surveilled all the known addresses including the boarding house at Lavender Bay. Lurie had two rooms there, 5A and 5B, out the back of the property. However, he was never there. The detective even went through his rubbish bins and reported, "Typical. Nothing but Chinese food containers and frangers. That's all there was."

It was Julian who came up with the idea of waiting for Lurie down by the ferry wharf. He figured Lurie would be expecting us at the boarding house and so we spent many a cold night waiting by the harbour for our man to appear. Ginger

Meggs and Billy Bunter on a stakeout. One glorious evening with the sun setting on Sydney Harbour, Lurie stepped off the ferry looking every bit the proverbial Sydney businessman: briefcase in hand, newspaper under arm and an affected air of self-importance. As he strolled past in a throng of commuters I walked up behind him and said, "Excuse me." He turned around and as he did I thrust the document into his hand. "You have been served," I barked, ensuring that I delivered the words exactly as instructed. A wave of horror and disbelief rippled across his face. It was astonishing. The first time in almost five years of dealing with this piece of work that he had ever displayed any reaction, any emotion of any kind. Out-foxed, out-smarted, out-manoeuvred. Julian came up beside me. Normally, process servers give you the document and then take off. Instead, we just stood there. He recovered his composure and gave us his 'you'll regret this' look. I resisted every urge to abuse the bastard and instead stayed silent. Then, he turned and walked. I felt that if ever there was a moment in this whole woeful saga where the Grey Blur had cause for pause, this was it. I'd like to think that it may have occurred to him then that he had misjudged terribly and gone after people who were not the sort of people you should ever mess with.

If up until this time we had been engaged in occasional hostilities with Lurie, it now became an all-out war. Of course, when you become embroiled in a war like this, the process of serving documents goes both ways. He also had to serve documents on us. On one occasion Julian and I were at North Sydney Court House just before a hearing. Lurie was sitting in one of the waiting-room chairs. He saw us walk in and Julian noticed that he had a form in his sweaty hands. Lurie walked over to us at which point Julian yelled at me, "Put your hands behind your back!" We both stood hands locked behind our backs. "You can't serve that in here, you fool," Julian castigated Lurie. "It has to be outside the courthouse." From the look on his face you could tell that Lurie knew this. After that we found a cosy little tearoom upstairs in the courthouse where we could wait for him to leave.

There is a rule that you cannot serve a document in the vicinity of a courthouse. One of the reasons is that no parties are to be surprised by an opposing party with new information on the day in court. Everyone has to have reasonable time to prepare their response to the other side's arguments in order for it to be a level playing field. It is amazing how the law has changed since then. Today, lawyers have been successful in serving via email, text messages and even on defendants' Facebook sites.

Lurie was one of those annoying people who never takes 'no' for an answer. He was unstoppable; as if being drowned in hot molten metal, or crushed in a massive machine press would not make the slightest difference. To me he seemed dead, like a vampire living on the blood of his victims. Nothing short of a silver bullet or a stake through the heart was going to finish him off. How many times had we heard senior judges say, "Mr Lurie, sit down. You have said enough."
"Yes Your Honour, but I would just like to point out…"
"Mr Lurie, sit down. I have finished hearing from you."

"But……"
"Mr Lurie, sit down!"
"Yes, but…"

During court one day, Julian and I somehow twigged that after the proceedings, Lurie was going to follow us out to serve something on us. I had followed Julian in the witness stand. I went back and sat next to him. By the time the magistrate wrapped up for the day Julian had already packed up his papers and both our bags. He whispered to me, "Come on. Let's go. I have your bag. We are out of here." I finally realised that we were doing a runner. Lurie was at the bar table. It was only a small courtroom so he was about four seats in front of us. As the magistrate said, "Thank you gentleman. Next case…" we raced out the door. Lurie realised what was happening and collected his things and ran after us.

We ran directly out onto the Pacific Highway with jackets and ties whipping in the wind. Fortunately, there was no traffic on the road and we shot straight across six lanes of highway and into the Northpoint Shopping Plaza. Like one of those scenes out of a Hollywood thriller we darted down the escalators, trying not to push over old ladies, out on to Miller Street, then jumped into a taxi and were out of there. Lurie-free. The adrenalin was pumping and there were high-fives all round. It was a really triumphant moment, which kind of shows how sad our lives had become.

Another classic serving scene occurred outside the New

South Wales Supreme Court in Phillip Street. Lurie followed us out of the building and was power walking up towards Julian and me. When I realised what he was doing, I sprinted across a pedestrian crossing leaving poor Julian for dead. Lurie decided to go after Julian with the document. Meanwhile, Julian ran into the little St James Church for sanctuary. He ran into the courtyard and came out the other side. I could see Julian getting to the fence and deliberating whether to go left down on to Elizabeth Street or go further down the fence. Lurie spotted him and it became a stand-off situation, like a child's game, if you run this way, I'll go that way. I was on the other side of the road watching this ridiculous farce where two grown men ran around in circles.

Because it is the Supreme Court, there are always lots of media packs waiting outside to get images of notorious criminals or celebrities before the courts. Lurie ran up to a television cameraman and barked at him, "Get this on camera, get this on camera. I am trying to serve this man and he keeps running away from me." It was hilarious to watch this cat-and-mouse game playing out on the Supreme Court surrounds. Fortunately, this madness wasn't deemed newsworthy and never made it to air.

CHAPTER SEVENTEEN

THE LITIGANT IN PERSON

Although we didn't have the best legal team money could buy, they were at least competent. Yet what frustrated me was that everything they assured me would not happen, in fact did happen. ITSA was an inconsequential organisation with less than twenty members constituted in such a way it was pointless taking legal action because it had no money or assets. When legal action was initiated we were confidently told it would be struck out. "What if it isn't struck out?" I enquired.

"No, that will never happen." So many people make the assumption that because you are presumed innocent the courts will look after you. Not only does it not work like that at all, the reverse is true. It didn't matter how much Julian and I protested that this was an abuse of process, the courts seemed determined to allow Lurie to do whatever he liked with impunity. The criminal, the fraudster, the scammer has a second choice, a third and a fourth choice. The victim doesn't have that. I don't know that the victim has anything. We turned to a lot of legal professionals for help, but not one of them could stop him.

One winter morning I walked into the court registry and filed a document which stated, "We, Alan Manly and Julian Day, the defendants, have terminated the authority of Gregory L. Donnelly to act as a solicitor for us in these proceedings." Then, I scribbled a note to our adversary. "Dear Mr Lurie, please find attached Notice of Intention to act without a solicitor, sealed by the court. Yours sincerely, Alan Manly." Such a significant step. Julian and I were going to defend ourselves. Although Greg 'Fatso' Donnelly had suggested this, it had now become imperative because I had been booted out of the college which up until then had been funding our defence. Now, we were well and truly on our own. Taking charge of our own defence changed everything for us. The pressure mounted as never before. If we lost, we would lose anything and everything we ever had. And yet if Lurie lost, he had nothing to lose.

Judges absolutely hate the litigant in person. One is a nightmare, two beyond the pale, and three is surely the last straw. With one litigant in person at least one of the brothers or sisters in the fraternity is getting some money. When both sides represent themselves, the profession misses out completely. By now Julian and I had been in a courtroom on an almost continuous basis for several years. So much had changed since this journey began. I was no longer the naïve fool with this schoolboy image of courtrooms being places where wise and learned men delivered considered and prudent judgment. That illusion had been well and truly shattered. I realised you could ignore judges, even be rude to them and it never made any difference. They reminded me of union shop stewards always keen to look after the interests of their comrades.

One of the solicitor's tricks I had picked up was to have plastic sleeves containing four copies of every document. When you have to hand them up to the bench, you can do it quickly and everyone gets a copy.

I stood at the Bar, as it is called, smouldering with indignation that I am there at all. Lurie stands. I noticed he looked the same as always, the man about town in a cheap suit. This distracted me and as I stood and placed my lever arch folder on the table somehow or other the front of the folder hit the desk and I watched in horror as all four copies of every document slid out of the sleeves and on to the courtroom floor.

We were off to a flying start with me crawling around on the floor scrambling for documents. It was very humiliating, being of near transparent skin, one or two steps away from albino, glowing bright red, and perspiring profusely. Lurie had been addressing the judge in his usual shambolic style and the judge had a look on his face which more than suggested he wondered what he had done to be put before this appalling mess.

The judge was not in a good mood. They never are, but this one may have had a reason. The case before mine was the infamous Mr Davidson. Whenever Davidson appeared in court it was wall-to-wall sheriffs. The judge read through Lurie's material muttering to himself, "Right, right, right." We all waited while the judge flipped through page after page. He was probably rattled after dealing with Davidson and now he had us.

Davidson was an architect from Baulkham Hills, the suburb next to where I resided. He is mad, or certainly madder than me. Maybe it is something to do with the water where we live. He operated his practice from his Baulkham Hills property until he decided his mortgage was unlawful. His reasoning came from the Magna Carta — the English legal charter of 1215. Essentially, Magna Carta was unique for its time because it stated that no one was above the law. Davidson's argument was that variable interest rates can't be a legally binding contract because contracts must provide 'certainty' and, by their nature, 'variable' interest rates are anything but certain. When interest rates climbed and his monthly mortgage payments doubled he stopped making repayments. The banks repossessed his property. He broke in and put all his office equipment back in place. When the banks took it all again, including his drawing boards and computers, Davidson reported the property stolen. He was charged and convicted of public mischief and trespassing, but sued the State Government for false imprisonment.

And I thought I was extreme in my views on the justice system. Davidson accused Nicholas Cowdrey, the Director of Public Prosecutions, of subverting the course of justice because Davidson subpoenaed three High Court judges and four Supreme Court judges whom he intended to cross-examine in the witness box. Davidson turned his repossessed Baulkham Hills property into a giant billboard where he wrote slogans about the banks, the courts and the government describing them as "thieving, killing, destructive and treasonous".

One day Davidson walked into court carrying a can of household paint. Why would you need a can of paint in court is a good question, but perhaps a better one is why anyone would let you into the court with a can of paint — this did happen before September 11. In a complete rage Davidson opened the can and threw paint over the judge. This is an incredibly dangerous thing to do. No one deserves that. It went all over the judge's face and he couldn't breathe. Everyone went into an absolute meltdown to keep the judge alive. Davidson could have accidentally killed him. There were sheriffs, cops and ambulance men everywhere. Davidson was arrested and locked up.

Since then, Davidson has been deregistered as an architect and in and out of prison for various acts of public mischief. He had various actions going against the State Government claiming that they were acting unconstitutionally. The word going round the courts was that Davidson was costing the government something like $40,000 a day in legal costs. "What a beast of a man," the lawyers concurred while they pocketed fabulous fees.

Davidson did stir my curiosity to actually read the Constitution of NSW, which is a bit of a worry. The NSW Constitution was written straight out of colonisation. Nothing has really changed terribly much since the days of the convicts. The Governor of NSW is actually a glorified prison governor. He, or she, can do anything. You can be locked up at the Governor's Pleasure in NSW forever. The courts mellow that and of course the Governor obliges the courts. But in actual fact the Governor can also delegate that authority to the Premier. The Governor can order a lock-down in NSW. After the paint-throwing affair, whenever Davidson appeared in court there were sheriffs everywhere.

At one point Lurie said, "I have some documents here which will explain my point."
"Very good," replied the judge, "bring them up."
At that, I rose to my feet behind the bar table the first time ever to address the court. This was a moment I could never forget. Bright red, dripping with perspiration, I said very politely, "Excuse me, Your Honour,"
"I will hear from you later," the judge replied dismissively.
"I would like to…."
"No, I will hear from you later — sit down!"
"Oh." So I sat down.

After about fifteen minutes reading to himself the judge looked up, then turned to me and said, "You wanted to say something?"
"I feel I have been denied natural justice," I stated.
"Why?"
"Well, you have read all those documents and you took some time to do it. You seem to have gone through them very thoroughly." I could see his face changing. I knew he knew what I was going to say next. "I have never seen those documents in my life, therefore I am unable to defend my-

self and you have been prejudiced against me."

If the judge was cranky when he climbed out of bed that morning, he was now in the realm of complete crack-up. Just for fun I even threw him a smile. He had survived a session with Davidson and now a mug like me with no legal training had trapped him. He went for Lurie and blasted him for misleading the court. The angrier he grew the calmer I became.

Sometimes I would ask myself, "How did I get into this situation?" There wasn't a choice. I didn't go looking for it. Lurie really went for Julian and me. Yet in a lot of ways Lurie liked Julian. They both seemed to thrive on the theatre of the courtroom whereas I just wanted Lurie to fuck off so I could have my life back.

I knew we only survived because there were two of us. Julian was more polished than I, but under that veneer of Billy Bunter's charming manners lay the British Bulldog. On weekends I read affidavits and pored over transcripts, prepared documents for filing, and read legal texts. Julian was better at filing documents with the court than me. Strategy was my best suit. I could dismantle an argument quite well, but whereas I was full of rat cunning, Julian was tenacious and able to follow four or five complex cases simultaneously and be perfectly calm. At times I could write a more solid defence than Julian, but he presented better in court. The judges liked him, but forced themselves to tolerate me. I was a working-class boy living a middle-class life in a two-storey house with a swimming pool and a rumpus room in the Bible belt in the north-west of Sydney. What more could a working-class boy ever want? I had been happy there until I lost my job. I now drove an eight-year-old car and most of the time it was a struggle to stay afloat financially.

A routine started to develop. Documents would arrive on a Friday. I'd spend the weekend going through them and preparing our defence. Monday and Tuesday nights were sleepless. I'd toss and turn in absolute sweats because we'd usually be in court on the Wednesday. That night I'd sleep from exhaustion. I seemed to be okay during the day, but at night, I would be overcome by such sadness. That's when I'd cry. The loneliness was so intense. I felt totally imprisoned. If it were not for Jennifer, this story would have a different ending. Like a Duracell bunny my mind ticks over 24/7. It's not that I don't relax, it's just that I constantly think about the next big issue in my life. I am very driven, and extremely opinionated, which means that sometimes I rub people up the wrong way. When that happens it doesn't bother me a bit. Jennifer jokes that I have the social skills of a fart. My response was that there was some truth in that, so long as the fart was silent, but deadly.

A kind person at the Registry had told Julian he should go down to the State Library and they would help him learn how to prepare documents for filing. We went down to the law department of the State Library, and the staff there showed us the process. It sounds very supportive and does make it is easier for everyone, but in some ways, it's like a legalised drug outlet — it supports the habit — it doesn't address the problem.

It wasn't long before Julian and I were recognised as solicitors and had registry clerks referring to us as solicitors. Court staff assumed we had many cases on and would occasionally say to us, "Are you fellows busy?"

Quite by chance I came across an article in *The Economist* on the inspirational Elisabeth Kubler-Ross who was famous for writing about how to deal with grief. Kubler-Ross's theory was that there were five stages of grief and as I read about this I realised that the horror story I was living was no different from a death in the family. I was dealing with the death of my freedom. The first stage you go through is denial. A summons would appear in my letterbox and I would say to myself, "You are kidding me. This can't be real." To your wife you say, "How ridiculous! They've even spelt my name wrong." You go to a solicitor and say, "This is preposterous!" I have never yet met a solicitor whose first reaction wasn't denial. "You are right, Mr Manly. This is ludicrous." Denial, denial, denial is their sales pitch.

Stage two is anger. "How can they do this to me?" When you get into court and your solicitor fucks it up they say, "Don't worry, if they are going to play it this way we'll bring in a barrister. Next time we'll wheel in the big guns."

The next stage is bargaining. "Maybe we can get out of it." We did make offers and there were counter-offers, but all for nought. Depression is the fourth stage. I found that particularly hard to shake. I was depressed for about ten years.

The last stage is stoic acceptance, which is very much the case when dealing with a death. Despite all of this happening, you have to get on with your life. I think Julian and I progressed to the stage of stoic acceptance quite early on. We even started to think it was perfectly normal that we spent most of our days in court arguing points of law. Didn't everyone do this? I latched onto the five stages of grief as it gave me a framework for understanding what was happening.

Obviously, Lurie had a major impact on our careers and personal lives. My business life was affected, my earning capacity nose-dived. Many times I considered giving up. I was even advised that the best thing I could do was disappear and move to another state. Really, two things kept me going: the support of my friend Julian Day, and a deep-rooted survival instinct. No one had to tell me that I was fighting for my life.

Julian and I developed a modus operandi to survive. We would meet an hour before the hearing at Carruthers Café, outside the court building. It was one of those shabby Sydney cafés with wobbly tables and rickety chairs. It was cramped and crumbling and like all of us had seen better days. The furniture was stuffed, but the tables were large and we could spread our documents out on them. Although the food was overpriced, the coffee was cheap, especially when the café served as a poor man's barrister's chambers. We were before the courts for so long, we actually saw that café go through three owners. At the café we would go over what had to be done, check our documents and decide who would act this time. Julian and I took turns passing the baton.

A couple of days after the Anzac Day holiday, Julian and I met up at Carruthers. Things were not good. "I don't want to do this any more," he said, sending a chill through me. He explained that his usual Anzac Day routine was to be there for the dawn service at the Drummoyne cenotaph after which he would head off to the RSL in Victoria Road. For breakfast he'd have three or four schooners and basically write the whole day off including, I suspect, himself. This year, Julian had been determined to do something different. He'd recently split from one of his wives or girlfriends and the pressure of our court cases was getting to him. As anticipated he was there for the dawn service and then back at the RSL. However, after one schooner he said to his chums, "See you, guys. I'm out of here." Everyone was taken aback. "Where are you off to?"
"I'm walking to Wollongong," Julian announced. True to his word he walked through the suburbs of Sydney down to Cronulla, caught the ferry across to Bundeena, and camped for the night on Burning Palms Beach in the National Park. The next day he walked the rest of the National Park, down Stanwell Tops, and along all the absolutely spectacular beaches of Austinmer and Coledale. He camped overnight

at Bulli and on the Sunday arrived in Wollongong where he had a couple of beers and then caught the train back.
"All I wanted to do was enjoy a long walk, see some great scenery and clear my head." It left him feeling exhilarated, but reminded him that there was more to life than battling Lurie. The collateral damage had been terrible for him: two marriages in ruin and his career was suffering.

There had been occasions in the past when one of us would be deeply depressed and the other had the strength to fight on, but this was different. Julian explained that he was torn between letting me down and his fear that if he fought on he might well find himself going insane. What could I say?

I picked up the baton that day and appeared before the Supreme Court. In the proceedings we clocked up yet another win against Lurie. Afterwards, as I walked along Phillip Street I rang Jennifer on the mobile and told her the good news of my win. "It just won't end will it? I just wish it'd all go away." She sounded despondent. What if I lost her? This case alienated everybody. I just couldn't talk about it to anyone any more. If they heard about it once more, they would scream themselves hoarse. Many different emotions swirled around inside me. There was anger, a helpless rage, and the sheer loneliness of my situation depressed me. Like Julian, I walked and I walked, down street after street, trying to keep it all together. Instead of becoming calmer, the anger grew. I realised my brother's warning was perceptive. I wondered how many others in the court system shared my predicament. The lyrics of Johnny Cash's song *I Walk the*

Line, came into my head.

I keep a close watch on this heart of mine
I keep my eyes wide open all the time
I keep the ends out for the tie that binds
Because you're mine,
I walk the line

This really was a life-and-death struggle. If Lurie was successful that would be the end for us. To keep it all together, I had to walk the line.

CHAPTER EIGHTEEN

WORMS AND NEMATODES

After being humiliated in court by Mark Gatehouse, and having lost control of the college, I was now unemployed. In the aftermath I always referred to this as my 'Losing the College' period. The pay-out wasn't overly substantial. My involvement in the legal stoush with Lurie probably meant I was unemployable, and I wanted to do something entirely different. I kept reminding Jennifer that a lot of successful businessmen were people who had left their professional careers and entered into totally new areas of which they knew absolutely nothing.

It was around this time that James, our son, who was by now in Year 10, started complaining of severe shoulder pain. We took him to our GP who did various tests and after six months of this he was still in pain. Another doctor in the same practice ordered a whole raft of new tests. Then she sent him to an orthopaedic surgeon who ultimately referred him to a neurosurgeon. The diagnosis was that his shoulder pain was caused by his brain herniating into his spine. He had developed scoliosis in his back. Michael Besser, one of the top neurosurgeons in the country, did the operation. James was in intensive care for forty-eight hours and spent six days in hospital. To be fair, Linda, his mother, came over from Adelaide for that. We were all there at the hospital: me, my partner, my ex-wife and my mother-in-law. You can imagine how anxious we all were. Then to my amazement, my ex-wife and mother-in-law bonded and became extremely friendly. Go figure. Dr Besser said that if we hadn't caught it when we did, James would have ended up a quadriplegic. Because he had to have this operation, James never sat for his School Certificate. Although the surgery was a success he will never regain some functionality he lost, but now stands upright with only a slight curvature of the spine. James went through all of this without ever complaining. The boy had such spirit. This time I spent with him and Jennifer reminded me all over again how their faith in me kept me going. I could only reward that loyalty by keeping on the straight and narrow and see my battle with Lurie through to the end.

I was sitting at the dinner table one night and Jenny's mother was down, which was a rarity in itself. As was my habit, I scanned the classifieds in the newspaper before dinner. My eyes pored over the list of businesses for sale when something caught my eye. "Now that's an idea," I announced enthusiastically.

"What?" Jennifer asked while standing over the boiling pots on the stove.

"Worm farming."

"Oh no," she moaned. She and her mother looked at me as though I had completely lost my marbles. Perhaps I had. I suspect Jennifer had been keeping a close eye on me ever since I had lost the college court case.

From nowhere I had this rush of blood to the head where I thought the environment would be the way to go. People were worried about saving the planet from environmental disaster. Surely I could do something and maybe even create a business at the same time. Needless to say I knew absolutely nothing about worm farming. Despite the new bravado and having been very critical of idiots who went off and started businesses they knew nothing about, I did exactly that. I drove around the north-west area of Sydney where I lived scouting for an appropriate site for a worm farm and came across this property on Showground Road in Castle Hill. It was an old, derelict chicken farm with buildings on it which had been abandoned when the business went bust.

I built up the long beds that needed to be raised above the ground and into them I laid a combination of soil and manure and threw in the worms. The product you are after is the worms and their vermicast; vermi is Latin for worm and cast being Latin for shit. It is an extremely rich soil fertiliser that is beautifully pure. The beds had to be kept at a certain temperature and needed a special watering system. As the worms grew and multiplied, we harvested them by the million and sold them by the kilo. Our trading name was 'Vinthrop' and during the early days, I realised there was an obvious need of an apparatus that would separate the worms from the soil without hurting them. For months, I became a mad, would-be inventor out in the carport at night, designing what ended up being a large steel contraption with a motor. You placed the soil in it and the worms

would just drop out the bottom.
I guess any self-respecting psychologist could have a field day with this stuff. It was as far away from the courtroom or the boardroom that I could get without going completely native and becoming a hippie or something. It was a simple, uncomplicated business which made people happy. They put worms in their gardens, and the lawns and plants bloomed. The world was a better place.

During the time I ran the college I had met a fellow called Paul Newman who owned a college in Bondi. We had a computer college and he had an English college so from time to time we bumped into each other at industry functions. I once made the mistake of accompanying Newman through Thailand and Indonesia as we were both trying to drum up business there. Even though I had a reputation for running a tight ship when it came to cost control, Newman was in another league altogether. For this trip he arranged the accommodation and we ended up in this hovel on the edge of Chinatown in Jakarta. It was a pretty ordinary place. He invited me to his room for a drink. The moment I walked in, I noticed this towel on the carpet beside the bed. I took a sniff. "Paul, this room doesn't smell so good".
"No," he replied matter of factly, "the sewerage pipe's leaking. I've put a towel down so it isn't so wet in here."
"Newman, are you really this broke?"
He said, "It's not that I'm broke, but they gave me this room on the cheap."
"That's because it smells like shit."
"Oh, not really, you just open a window."

"You can't," I replied, "the mosquitoes will come in and you'll end up with malaria."

"No, the mossies hide behind the wardrobe. So I close the door and move the wardrobe over and swat them one by one." The guy was unbelievable.

After one of our trips Jennifer and I had Newman and his wife over for a barbeque. Our wives were chatting and Jennifer casually mentioned that although she didn't like me being overseas so much, at least she took some comfort that I phoned home every day.

"But not from Asia?" his wife asked. "The phones are atrocious."

Jennifer agreed that the lines were so often crackly and full of static that she would joke when she answered, "Is that you, E.T?"

"So Alan rings you every day?"

"Yes," Jennifer replied.

There was total silence from Newman's wife, who was a GP and no fool. Then, using her best bedside manner she elicited from Jennifer the fact that I rang no matter where I was. Vietnam was especially memorable. All the phones were bugged. Occasionally they left the line open and you could hear the secret police chatting as they ate their lunch with Radio Hanoi on in the background. Poor Newman was suddenly looking unwell. Later, he confided that he was aghast that Jennifer had mentioned my calls home. "Have you any idea what it costs to ring from overseas?" he moaned. "Now I'll have to ring home every day."

ONE ONE FIVE

One day after I had left the college business Newman rang me. "Mate, I've met this guy whose looking for partners to buy this really interesting business operating out of Macquarie University. It's in administration and this guy, Barry Toohey, reckons we could buy it." I had nothing much on my plate; the worms were more or less running the business and I was feeling a bit lost and lonely and sad. A meeting was organised.

Toohey looked like a burnt-out alcoholic which was pretty much what he was. He was shorter than me, clean shaven with pretty much a full head of hair, but going grey. I remember that he would never do up his shirt collar, never did the cuffs up either, so they used to flap around which I found annoying. He'd been on the wagon for a few years and was now a fanatical non-drinker. Barry loved a good meal, but would never eat dessert because of the risk of accidentally ingesting alcohol. Having been a chain-smoker knocking over a couple of packets of Camel a day, he had this deep, gravelly voice which could talk under wet cement. Toohey had had a very interesting corporate career with General Motors in America. From there he'd gone into advertising and boasted he was best mates with lots of famous people. According to Toohey, Nemax, a company which had been placed in administration, was the classic licence to print money. "You don't know how lucky you are," he enthused. "We're going to make millions."

The head office Nemax operated from what had once been an old cottage, commonly known as the fungus factory, located on the campus of Macquarie University. This arrangement meant Nemax were able to use the magical address of the university which gave it enormous credibility, even though it was an independent company with no association with the university. As well as that, Nemax had a research station located in the Philippines from where its scientists were developing a solution to the world-wide problem of nematodes. Nematodes? Well, I had not heard of them before either.

If the roses in your garden have ever looked really sad, the gardener will most likely tell you that the nematodes have got them. Nematodes only attack introduced plants in Australia such as grapes and wheat. They are tiny little critters which live under the ground and at a size of around 10-^{11} (0.000000000001 mm) impossible to see with the naked eye. In a microscope they look like very cute baby dinosaurs. They are all head and mouth and eat the furry bits of roots. Nematodes travel underground and when they infest plants the results can be devastating. Australia loses about ten per cent of its wheat crop to nematodes. The wine industry suffers similarly. A professor had happened to notice that when people threw something out of the laboratory window the tomato plants under the window thrived. Tomatoes are an introduced plant from South America. Why didn't the nematodes attack those tomatoes? One thing led to another and this professor made a miraculous discovery that this rapacious fungus could destroy the nematodes. Nemax was trying to commercialise the solution to this problem by developing a nematicide which was based on this fungus.

This fungus would attack the nematodes in the ground. The product which had been used for this problem in the past, DDT, had been banned because of its dangerous long-term side-effects. A solution to the nematode problem was destined to make millions.

Toohey was an unusual fellow. I recall that one of his goals was to retire to the Swiss Alps in three or four years and write his life story. He asked me about my background. Having counselled myself not to mention under any circumstances my legal stoush with Mark Gatehouse and to never ever utter the poisonous words Elliott Lurie, I did exactly that. Like a man possessed I somehow found myself pouring out my heart and soul about how I was being screwed over by the legal system and the more glassy-eyed my audience became the more I gave it to them. There was a deathly silence at the end and much looking at watches. I realised I had prattled on far too long and said to Toohey and Newman, "How bad was that?"
"Yeah, that was bad," Barry agreed, "but by God, I do love the mad Irishman in you."

The three of us agreed to try and buy Nemax from the administrators. Toohey would look after the sales side of the enterprise and I was confident he could do that. From what I could make of him, his only bad habit was that he was a shameless name-dropper, claiming to be personal friends with people like Jack Cowin, the fast-food billionaire. At least with Newman there was comfort in the fact that when you went into business with him you didn't ever have to worry about any extravagant expenditure.

We went to the first creditors' meeting. There were about fifty people there. The administrator made an announcement. "Now if any of you folks here aren't on the creditors' list and you wish to make a claim, just come forward and give me some evidence of a claim and I'll add you to the creditors' list." Toohey wandered up to the administrator and said, "I'd like my name added to the creditors' list."

"Certainly, sir. What's the name?"

"Barry Toohey."

"Right. And what's the amount?"

"Seventy-five dollars."

"Right. And what would that be for?" the administrator enquired.

"Reimbursement of parking," Toohey replied deadpan.

"When would that have been?"

"About the last week they were trading," explained Toohey.

"That would be ... when was it?"

The administrator helpfully replied, "Well, we were appointed the first of June, so that'd be around 25 May? Okay. And have you a receipt?"

"No," Toohey responded, "I didn't get the receipt."

"Well and good," the administrator said, and added Barry Toohey as one of the creditors.

As Toohey took his seat the administrator looked at us. "Yes?" he asked. "What are you owed?"

"Well," Newman mumbled, "I lent this director called Peter Horton $200." Then he turned and looked at me. "And half of that was yours, right?"

"That's right," I spluttered. The administrator added us to

the list of creditors. We took seats next to the man from Canberra who represented the government department of regional development or whatever, who were owed about $400,000. That's the crazy thing about this process. Every creditor has one vote. Toohey who is supposedly owed $75 has one vote, Newman and I who are allegedly owed $200 between us have two votes and the man next to us who is owed close to half a million gets one vote. However, if there is disagreement and a poll is requested, then the vote is based on dollars owed.

There is a well-worn ritual to these meetings. At the first creditors' meeting you have a roll up of about fifty creditors, and they're all baying for blood. Almost invariably, the most vocal demands are made from those owed the least. After much yelling and screaming, the administrator announces that the cupboards are bare and basically they can kiss their money goodbye. The creditors then troop out sullen and depressed and angry having done their dough. Stage one of the five stages of grief.

By the time of the second creditors' meeting only about five turn up. These are the die-hard optimists plus the man from Canberra who seems a picture of passivity. The directors are missing in action. The money is all gone and the remaining assets worthless. The only hope is if some fool would buy the business. It is at this point that Toohey begins negotiations with the administrators to buy Nemax.

Seemingly from thin air the sum of $21,000 appears on the

radar. How did they come up with that figure? My suspicion is that it closely correlated to what would be the administrators' fee. I suppose that's how these things work a lot of the time. The creditors lose everything, and the only party paid anything are the administrators who have been sent in to see what could be salvaged from the wreckage. In this case, all that could be salvaged was their fee. The administrator was prepared to let it go for $21,000, but wanted assurances on the money.

Armed with my cheque book I produced a cheque for $7,000 and handed it over. I noticed that Newman gave his cheque grudgingly, like he had sold one of his children into slavery. With a flourish, Toohey tossed his cheque to the administrator. The company was ours. As we were walking down the hallway Toohey whispered, "Mate, you couldn't stand us for seven grand, could ya?" He explained that there was no money in his account and if I couldn't cover for him the cheque would bounce. If Toohey was such great mates with a billionaire why did he need to borrow from me? Hmmmm? Firm promises were made to pay it back no later than the end of the week, but even by the end of the decade, my loan was still outstanding. Meanwhile, Newman was walking in front of us and I could hear him on his mobile saying to someone, "No, it's a joint bank account. I'm allowed ... it's a joint bank account." So it was in these rather inauspicious circumstances that I became one of the joint managing directors of Nemax. Even though the business had never turned a profit despite the millions pumped into by the government, we thought it was a bargain. I sold my worm business and was now in the nematode game.

CHAPTER NINETEEN

'HE WHO SEE THROUGH STEEL'

The impression we soon picked up was that Nemax had been a dream place to work, which no doubt explained why it had gone broke. The professors on the payroll would take themselves off to Manila and after swanning around there head off down south to Davao where the research facility was located. I guess if you were into biology then the Philippines was a very interesting place. One of my tasks was to put the whole business on a commercial footing and the frugality of the new owners came as a shock. Even I was amazed with Newman's tight-fistedness. On one occasion we were suited up to go to an important meeting when he opened up a can of paint and started painting the walls of our office. "Newman, what are you doing?"

"We can do this while we wait," he explained. "We've got half an hour."

"Paul, you can't be serious. We'll have paint all over us. We'll stink of turps," I protested, but he took no notice. It didn't worry him in the slightest.

One of the first things we had to do was get up to the Philippines to sort out what was happening there. The most damaged crops due to nematodes are banana plantations and the company was running a research project on a plantation there.

Newman and I flew to Manila and caught a light plane to Davao, on one of the southern islands of the Philippines. After we'd been flying for an hour over banana plantation after banana plantation, like a kid I asked, "Are we there yet?" The pilot turned around and very dryly remarked, "We've been here for at least fifteen minutes," meaning we'd been flying over the plantation we were going to for all that time. The smallest banana plantation in the Philippines is bigger than all of the banana plantations in Australia combined.

A four-wheel drive picked us up at the airstrip and we drove off to the main plantation compound. As we were bouncing along, the driver noticed a road block across the road ahead. One of our guides picked up something from the floor, turned to me and said, "Quick. Get under the blanket." When I looked at him strangely he explained, "This isn't a police road block. These are Muslim terrorists." They figured that the Muslims wouldn't like to see our white, seemingly Christian faces.

It wasn't long before I realised why we were here. The 'odd' problem at the research station was in fact an unholy mess. The scientists employed by the former owners were among the best in the world. I have not the slightest doubt that they were truly brilliant. The tragedy was that although most of them had the best of intentions, they were slowly, but inexorably exposed to every temptation on offer in the Philippines. When I met one of our scientists, Dr Zillman, at breakfast, he was drunk. He boasted to me that he was world famous, but I replied sadly that I had never heard of him.

It transpired that he would start drinking at around seven in the morning and by lunchtime he'd be roaring drunk. This would go on for another good twelve hours. He would collapse during meetings and snore his head off. His nickname in Tagalog was 'ang taong ay laging lasing', or, 'the one who is always drunk'. The good doctor wore that nom de plume like a badge of honour.

Dr Zillman was one of those characters torn from the pages of a Graham Greene novel. Zillman had married a local girl, which can be an advantage, of course. As well as contacts, it gives you insight into local customs and culture. Apparently, he went to the Australian embassy as a guest and met her there. She was an assistant cleaner. How impressed must the Filipinos have been. If you're a Westerner picking up girls, at least pick up one who's had an education. His wife was cleaning the toilets in the Hilton Hotel, so that was more baggage for our business. He was quite a learned soul, but the good doctor had gone native and managed to upset many of the locals. As he distributed all the cash they saw him as the boss man and he lorded it over them.

On those rare occasions when he was sober, Dr Zillman was shy and timid. If you spent ten minutes talking to him you could not but admire what a marvellous mind he had. However, when loaded, he became a real monster. He could speak some Tagalog and abused all and sundry in that language. He played favourites, involved himself in local politics and concerned himself with everything other than what he had been sent there to do. There were no financial controls. Research money was being spent to pay off locals and to buy alcohol. Also, the efficacy of the chemical testing was debatable as the data was handled by drunks and I had some suspicion they might be enhancing the results, rendering them meaningless. The more I saw the more I came to the conclusion that this was an unmitigated disaster.

The plantation was massive and the workers were viewed by the owners as being nothing more than peasants. There were people who had never left the plantation in all their lives. They considered themselves lucky to be allowed to live on the property. It was unabashed feudalism. The local priest doubled as the village witchdoctor. One day this priest turned up with a couple of local lads who'd found a gold nugget up in the hills. It was as big as your fist and there was much excitement over the discovery. Dr Zillman examined the nugget and then announced to the priest and the others that it was actually fool's gold. I thought this discovery most apt. The entire place was nothing but fool's gold.

One of the first problems I encountered was the issue of the missing company seal. For lots of complicated local legal requirements I won't go into, contracts could not be renewed without being stamped by the company seal, but no one could find it. The former directors had secured it somewhere, but no one could remember where and it was presumed lost. Replacing the seal in the Philippines was a nightmare scenario. Obviously, the first place to look was the office. Then it became apparent that no one actually knew if we had an office, or if we did where it was. After making some enquiries I was directed to the local airport. It turned out that there was a Filipino investor who was a director of the local subsidiary. It was a wobbly sort of arrangement, but somehow manageable. He owned one or two passenger aircraft and a couple of crop dusters and was responsible for the current DDT spraying program. He used to air freight us around the place a bit and had visions of securing the rights to spray our product using his crop dusters. The 'office' consisted of nothing more than five four-drawer filing cabinets stashed in a corner of one of the aircraft hangers.

I wasn't put off by the fact that the missing company seal for the Philippines subsidiary hadn't been found despite numerous searches. Instead of looking through all the filing cabinet drawers I sat in the office and said to myself, "Now, if this was a white man's office, where would one hide the company seal?" I thought, "Not the filing cabinet closest to the door, and not the one furtherest from the door. Perhaps that cabinet." Then I thought, "Not the top drawer, not the bottom. Try the third from the top." I opened the filing cabinet, looked around in the third drawer and there it was — the company seal. Indisputably, that was the only useful thing I did in all the time I was a director of Nemax. Thereafter Toohey, who had a great turn of phrase, referred to me as 'he who see through steel'. The locals loved it too and gave me that nickname in Tagalog, 'sa kanya sino makita sa pamamagitan asero'; 'he who see through steel'.

The product currently used on the plantation for the

nematode problem was manufactured by a pharmaceutical company and was essentially DDT in another form. The Filipino workers were supplied with a spacesuit to protect them from the chemicals and because they were paid danger money to spray the trees they fought each other for the right to wear the spacesuit. When I went out to where they were working I saw the man wearing the spacesuit going around the banana palms using this little pump to spray the plants. He was fully protected from the chemicals except that he wasn't wearing any shoes. Any scientist worth his salt will tell you that the fastest way to absorb chemicals into the body is through the skin via the webbing on your toes and your hands. After that I started noticing that some of the kids on the plantation appeared to have deformities.

Within metres of my hotel room people lived in the most awful squalor. The humidity in the place was unbelievable. I was someone who dripped with perspiration in an air-conditioned courtroom. Here, my clothes simply rotted away after a couple of days. Everything was green. I'd never seen so many shades of green. This was not a good period in the life and times of Alan Manly. How had I ended up in a place like this? Was this some misguided mistake to escape from the courtroom dramas that were consuming my life? I was a young man full of ideas and energy who had somehow lost his way. It was difficult for me to see how I could get my life back on the rails. Were it not for my wife and son, who had such faith in me, I don't know what would have become of me.

It became my sad and solitary duty to have words with the Dr Zillman. I waited for a time when he was sober, and when that opportunity did not avail itself, picked the moment when I thought he was less out of control than normal. As diplomatically as I could, given the heat, and the insects, and the hopelessness of it all, I tried to persuade him that we needed to put the project on a sound commercial footing. Although it was apparent that the investors were being ripped off left, right and centre I kept my cool and hoped that I could convince him that change was needed. However, he would have none of it and within minutes our discussion had degenerated into a slanging match. I told the good doctor what I thought of his research station and challenged the validity of the scientific testing. Zillman took great umbrage at these claims and demanded that I apologise. Ratso wouldn't apologise. Instead I told him that he should be apologising for blowing the investors' money. The doctor called in some of the Filipinos standing around casually who pretended that they hadn't been listening to this blazing row. Speaking in Tagalog Zillman told them something of what I was saying and the locals, knowing he was the source of the money, affected great outrage. I did feel that at any minute I might be beheaded by the natives, or placed in a very large cooking pot and boiled for their supper. Naturally, Zillman was all puffed up by the reaction of the locals and angrily accused me of being a miserable bean counter. "Now fuck off, you miserable cunt," he screamed, much to the amusement of the locals.

The next morning Newman came in to my room and asked,

"Well, what are you going to do?"
"I'm going home," I replied.
"Oh, no. You've got to go down there and apologise to Dr Zillman."
"Mate, they're a bunch of crooks," was my response. To my amazement Newman had this 'so what' look on his face, that we should not be surprised to find ourselves up to our armpits in corruption. "I'll tell you what, Paul. If you want my share of the business I'll sell it to you."
"Really?"
"Seven thousand dollars. Okay? My original stake."
"Okay," he replied and we shook hands on the deal.

So I left Davao, made my way to Manila, and flew back to Sydney. Not long after I arrived home the phone rang. It was Barry Toohey. "Where are you?" he wanted to know.
"You just rang my phone, at home. Where do you think I am?"
He started to laugh. "Well, mate, Newman thinks you're still in your hotel room sulking?"
"Really?" I replied.
"Yeah, he rang me and said that you hadn't come out of your room for three days. He'd tried to ring you but you never answered the phone. He's worried that he might have said something to upset you."
"Upset me? I sold him my shares in the business."
"No talking you out of it?" Toohey asked in a half-hearted fashion.
I realised that if I badmouthed the business too much there was less likelihood that I would get my money from New-

man. Of course Toohey still owed me $7,000 for his part of the original deposit, but that subject was conveniently avoided.

When Newman returned from the Philippines he came around and paid me out. I was out of the nematode business. Several years later I ran into Paul Newman who told me the investors did their dough big time and ended up all suing each other over their interests in the intellectual property. He said so much money was eaten up on legal fees that by the end there was nothing left for the victors. This was a familiar refrain.

And so my 'green period' as my wife Jennifer described it, came to an end. Nemax was a bitter blow for me. I had been so desperate for it to succeed. Again I found myself unemployed and unemployable. For one brief moment I had been like Superman, the man who could see through steel. I was clever, I was capable, I was ambitious, but it was all was-was-was like this had been me in another life and now I was riddled with self-doubt. Perhaps this instinctive desire to work for myself, to run my own business, was just folly. Day by day I felt that life was passing me by. I was by now in my forties well and truly and had nothing. With time on my hands I rummaged through my memories searching for the so-called tipping point, the moment where it all started going south instead of north. Only one word ever bubbled up from the graveyard of my past: Lurie. Had I made a mistake taking him on? Would it end with me being declared the victor and my prize a career in absolute ruins. If there was indeed a highway to hell, like the famous song declared, then I must have been travelling on the autobahn to oblivion.

CHAPTER TWENTY

SCENES FROM A STAIRWELL

I walked into Carruthers Café to load myself up with caffeine for the next round with Lurie and sitting there at a table was my grinning, pudgy friend, Julian Day. We shook hands. It seemed like a lifetime ago since we had last met. Over coffee he told me what was happening in his life. Julian had told Ricki about his Sydney to Wollongong walk, and she then encouraged him to do another one, this time from Wollongong to Huskisson on the South Coast. For his second walk he was a lot more organised. He worked out his route, talked to rangers and people from the local councils and as only Julian can, lined up a sponsor. At the time he was doing some IT work for the St George Bank and they agreed to put in a couple of thousand dollars, all of which he donated to the NSW Cancer Council. When I asked why he selected them as his charity of choice Julian paused and then said, "Because I'm a cancer survivor." As that was sinking in he added, "Three times."

He told me that when he was about eighteen months old, his parents noticed him limping as he walked down the steps of his grandmother's house. The local GP sent them to a Harley Street specialist who diagnosed a granuloma tumour in the hip. Julian had surgery and radiotherapy and was hospitalised for about nine months. The condition reappeared in his left shoulder when he was about six, and in the right shoulder blade at the age of ten. He has vivid memories of being the bald-headed boy at school. "That's why this shit with Lurie is just child's play to me. Having beaten cancer, I can survive anything." His walk to Huskisson along some of the greatest beaches was a terrific success. He managed to raise quite a bit of money for the Cancer Council and was nominated for a civic award.

In recognition of his contribution to charities, Julian was given the honour of carrying the Olympic torch through his home suburb. I was there by the roadside in Drummoyne at five in the morning and Ratso is not a morning person. But it was a real accolade for him to be given the public recognition of running the torch through the streets of his local community. After he passed on the Olympic torch, Julian then went from pub to pub, still in his torch bearer's uniform and the publicans shouted him drinks all day and through the night.

It occurred to me then that I may have seriously misread Julian. I'd always pegged him as Billy Bunter, but I wasn't so sure any more. He didn't have any trouble reading my mind. Just as I was wondering if he was back on board he said to me in his unmistakeable deadpan way, "Checked the court list in the paper. Saw we were on. Thought you might need a hand."

To begin bankruptcy proceedings, Julian and I, the creditors, had to file a Creditor's Petition asking the Court to make a Sequestration Order in respect to the estate of the Debtor,

Lurie. The petition could only be presented if Lurie had committed an act of bankruptcy in the previous six months. But first we had to find him to serve the documents.

Through making a copious number of phone calls using some clever pretexts, Julian and I established that Lurie was working out of an office in Crows Nest. It was one of those three-storey buildings which didn't have a lift. Around midday Julian and I opened the door and climbed a steel staircase up to Lurie's supposed place of employment. Being pretty wound up in those days, we stormed into the office on the top floor and asked the receptionist, "Is Elliott Lurie here? We are here to serve some bankruptcy documents."

"Oh, oh, bankruptcy?" she whimpered. "He's out right now."

The office itself was like a business version of his boarding house room — pokey, cheap and threadbare. There was no where to hide. Even so, it was remarkable the man had an office at all.

Deflated that we couldn't find him, we headed back down the stairs. As we reached the first level, we heard an icy voice from above. "There you are." We both looked up. Lurie was standing at the top of the stairs looking down. He was in an absolute rage. Not only had we discovered he was operating a business, but we had dropped the word 'bankruptcy' like a hand grenade in his office. Lurie slowly descended eyeballing Julian who was standing at the bottom of the stairs. Then he saw me and went insane. Julian was the reasonable face whereas I was the unacceptable face of the enemy. He pushed Julian to one side and started punching me with his fists. This completely took us by surprise. The only confrontation we expected was between him and Julian as he had really wanted the pleasure of serving Lurie with the bankruptcy notice. Instead, Julian was knocked to one side and a shower of fists slammed into my head. Being a poor, white trash boy from Bacchus Marsh, I knew how to handle myself in a blue. The temptation to retaliate was incredible. I was taller, stronger and fitter.

I knew enough about survival to know that the best defence in this situation was to go into a huddle, make myself as small a target as possible, and keep my fists to myself. It even occurred to me that if this idiot persisted with this assault he might just end up in the slammer. I noticed my bursting-at-the seam briefcase bouncing down the stairs and then I realised I was bouncing down the stairs as well. When I hit the landing I tried to get up on all fours, but I was pummelled, bashed and kicked. I clung to the railing of the staircase for dear life. Julian kept yelling, "Back off, you bastard," and did what he could to try and pull Lurie off me, but he just wouldn't let go. I heard Julian on his mobile calling the police. He gave me a few more thumps, but with the police on their way he knew the game was up. "Next time, I will fucking kill you," Lurie screamed.

It was then that Julian did something which made me immensely proud. Never one to miss an opportunity he walked up to the furious Lurie and served him the bankruptcy notice. "You have been served," he said with a matter-of-fact voice before Lurie bolted back up the stairs. Seeing him being served brought me a lot of joy even while I was semi-concussed.

After being treated at the local hospital, we then found ourselves back at the police station where it all began. Even though most of the coppers we had dealings with had moved on, we were still legends at that station. We were welcomed back like a couple of citizen sheriffs. You would swear our photos were framed and proudly displayed on a wall somewhere. Certainly, Lurie was burned into their memory banks. One look at my face and they knew I had been assaulted. Photographs were taken, statements typed up and in a replay of what had happened so many years before out went a squad car with sirens blaring to arrest Lurie. I was almost overcome by a profound sense of déjà vu. Hadn't we been through all this before?

Later, we deduced that when we called at the office in Crows Nest, Lurie had probably been upstairs in the toilet. He definitely knew we were in the building and when he came looking for us he was stark-raving-mad-angry. I think what most infuriated Lurie was himself. He had gone to such lengths to conceal his business operation and we had busted him big time.

When I was given notice of the hearing, I wrote a letter to the court and explained that as I had been assaulted by Lurie I wanted assurances regarding my personal safety. I refused to attend court unless I had protection. As I had anticipated, none was forthcoming. Knowing the court system as I did, I just knew that my letter would have been copied and filed, but no one would have actually read the damned thing. The assault case was heard in the North Sydney Local Court. When I arrived at court I was dismayed by the absence of security. There was no security screening at all. The court was wide open. You could have walked in with a machine gun and no one would have known. I noticed there was an old and overweight sheriff loitering about who looked like he was minutes away from cardiac arrest. Before long, my nemesis arrived on his own. No doubt he would represent himself. There were just the two of us apart from the sheriff. I was never afraid of Lurie. He was not physically threatening to me, but I often worried about what went on in that head of his. He busied himself setting out his pens and documents on the bar table, like a waiter setting out a place for a diner. For a fleeting moment I thought about picking up the nearest chair and smashing it over him. That might liven things up. It infuriated me that Lurie made me think like this. Into my head popped the voice of my Baptist mother, "Proverbs 11:21. Truly the evil man shall not go unpunished, but those who are just shall escape." Even though I hadn't had a religious thought in decades, much less read the bible, there it was. Messages like land mines planted in the past and exploding in the subconscious when you triggered them in the heat of the moment.

Many times Julian and I asked ourselves, "Who is this guy?" Clearly, he was not your average Joe Blow. It occurred to me that Lurie might be a victim of his own game, but didn't realise this. Whatever was going on in that head of his, he was locked into a high-risk strategy.

Dissatisfied with the complete lack of security I spoke to the bailiff and warned him that I would bring in my security team if something wasn't done. "This man here has been charged with assaulting me," I thundered. "If you can't provide guards, I'll bring in my own." The bailiff shot a look over at Lurie and then a look to the sheriff who had momentarily nodded off on a chair propped up against the back wall. "I'll have a word with the magistrate," the bailiff promised and went off.

In the meantime, the police prosecutor arrived. It was the same woman who had gone for Lurie's jugular in his fraud conviction. She flashed me a smile and after a quick word she arranged for some police officers to be stationed in the courtroom in case there was trouble. The prosecutor had a certain zeal about her; almost as if she couldn't get to my assault case quick enough. If ever there was an unlosable case, this was it: photographs and hospital reports of a bruised and battered man; an accused with a motive; and an eyewitness. For an unprovoked assault like this I felt that a jail term was warranted. This was where the bastard ultimately belonged.

As both Julian and I were witnesses we didn't get to hear the evidence, but waited outside. While I waited my turn to give evidence, a business partner of Julian's walked out of the court. We started chatting and he mentioned that the police were worried that Lurie might get off scot-free because Julian's testimony varied from the account I had given in my statement. However, I thought the differences in our accounts added to our credibility, that we had not fabricated our evidence so that it was word perfect. Anyway, the prosecutor was determined to convince this dithering magistrate. She pointed out that our evidence was spot on for the critical issues of where, when and how, even if there was some variation on when the yelling and screaming started.

After hearing all the evidence the magistrate adjourned for about an hour to consider the matter and then returned informing the court that he had found Lurie guilty of assault as charged. The police prosecutor was fantastic. She described Lurie as a convicted fraudster and argued that he should be imprisoned for this unprovoked assault on another person who had shown remarkable restraint in the circumstances. Moreover, she argued the incident had happened when the victim was attempting to serve a court document on Lurie. His assault was also an attack on the court itself.

The magistrate asked Lurie for his response to the crown's submission and he informed the court that at the time of the incident he was depressed. Also, he had been provoked. With that the prosecutor leapt to her feet and pointed out that if anything the evidence was that there had been no provocation. As had happened so many times in the past I watched as the court swung into over-drive to look after the interests of the guilty. This was a blatant open-and-shut case, but again the victim played no part in determining the punishment of the perpetrator. The rights of the criminal outweigh those of the victim.

Even though not one single piece of evidence was provided to substantiate Lurie's claim of suffering from depression, the magistrate bought the package. Lurie was fined $400, ordered to pay me $400, and to cough up $640 for Julian's witness expenses. It was nothing short of outrageous and so perverse it was almost funny. A man being sued for bankruptcy who had not paid a cent in costs awarded against him in the past seven years had been given a fine. Of course Julian and I knew that even though we were awarded costs, these were dollars that we would never see in this lifetime. Our prosecutor told the magistrate in no uncertain terms that the punishment was manifestly inadequate, but to no avail. She turned to me and said, "I'm sorry. This man should be behind bars." However, there was one positive to come out of all this. The prosecutor explained that Lurie would never appeal. He couldn't appeal the verdict – the evidence was there in black and white. If he appealed his punishment, it was highly likely an appeal court would increase it and send him to jail.

Then we had to sit through the spectacle of Lurie pleading with the magistrate for more time to pay the fines. Finances were a bit tight at the moment, if he could pay in instalments that would make things a lot easier. Like two clowns playing tennis with an imaginary ball, back and forth it went, arguing over something everyone knew was never going to happen. Finally, the magistrate decided on a "fair and reasonable" fine payment plan and it was all over.

For some reason I believed I was inured to miscarriages of justice and was surprised with how upset I became that day. Public humiliation in the courts was my daily fare. Why should it have been any different this time? And yet I was shattered. I felt it was not physically possible for me to go on. A part of me wanted to cry out, "Okay. I give up. What do you fucking want?" I felt a hand on my shoulder and looked up. It was Julian.

"Are you all right?" he asked.

"Fine, I'm fine," I replied.

"You know," said Julian softly, "someone's going to die before this thing ends."

CHAPTER TWENTY-ONE

THE MAKING OF A BANKRUPT

An act of bankruptcy is a failure to comply with a bankruptcy notice or a failure to satisfy the Court there is a counter-claim. As you can imagine, Lurie always had a counter-claim.

Before the court could decide that Lurie was a bankrupt and make a sequestration order, it had to consider the truth of the allegations of the petition, whether the petition was served properly, whether the debt upon which the petition was based was still owing and whether it exceeded $2,000. If the court was satisfied, then it would issue a sequestration order. Immediately, the debtor becomes a bankrupt and his estate vests in the official trustee.

Although bankruptcy is a very serious situation, the modern interpretation in this country is that it is all terribly bad luck. In France it is a criminal offence and in Switzerland you go to prison. There were ironies aplenty. Here I was trying to bankrupt Lurie at the very time that my own financial situation was perilous in the extreme. I can attest that in the years that I wasn't employed, I didn't notice a single decline in any of our household expenses. They just kept rolling in. It was also difficult to secure employment because I had to spend so much time in court.

Thanks to interest Lurie now owed $44,515.16. On 30 April 1999, he filed an application under the *Bankruptcy Act 1966* seeking an order that the Bankruptcy Notice served on 23 August be set aside.

The New South Wales Court of Appeal dismissed Lurie's appeal of Judge Dillon's decision. Then on 13 September 1999, Master Morton, in the Supreme Court dismissed a summons which Lurie dressed up to be an appeal against Blackwood's assessment of costs. Morton also remarked that there was considerable animosity between the parties. He didn't know the half of it. Lurie was like a gambler. He kept betting his luck in the courts would cover his previous court costs.

In August 2000, we appeared before Justice Lawson in the Federal Court of Australia. Lawson wanted to know the basis of Lurie's appeal. When he started wandering all over the place, Lawson asked him for his 'best point' of appeal. The plaintiff stood up, and smoothed down his cheap tie. Invited to make his best point he then proceeded to make three. "Thank you, your Honour. These are the major issues. The first one, as I am sure you can appreciate, is a very serious matter, exceptionally serious, particularly in the case of myself being involved in a number of projects that concern a number of people."

Lawson was having none of it. "Your first point is that

bankruptcy is a serious matter?"
"Very serious," Lurie agreed, "and the affidavits I have provided explain that this is a very fast moving industry I am involved in. This bankruptcy notice was lodged over twelve months ago and in the last six to seven months a great deal has happened for me to be able to show the court that now I am in a position financially, not only solvent, but more importantly to explain to the court why this creditor's petition and bankruptcy notice should be dismissed."

"If you're solvent, why don't you pay the District Court judgment? Why don't you pay? What's the problem? You have exhausted all avenues of appeal and according to material that I have read on the file, you have no assets," Lawson argued.
Lurie replied, "May I point out, sir, first of all, the avenues of appeal which are mainly…"
"Just address my question," Justice Lawson demanded. "What is the basis for you saying you are solvent? What assets do you have?"
"The assets I have, your Honour, are intellectual property assets."
"What is the intellectual property?"
"The knowledge I have."

The judge sighed. Julian sighed as did I. "Mr Lurie, is there any possibility of you paying this $40,000?"
"Oh yes, your Honour," he lied. "I have only been asking for more time."
"Well, you have had some of that. What could I say to the

creditors here, to give them comfort that you wouldn't be wasting their time?"

"As you know," Lurie teased, "Bill Gates is coming to Australia next month and…"

"And?"

"He is in the IT industry."

"Yes," said the judge, rolling his eyes. "I am aware of who Bill Gates is."

"And so am I."

"So you are what?" the judge asked.

"So am I in the IT industry. The same industry as Mr Bill Gates."

"Really?"

"Yes, yes," Lurie enthused. "Now I don't want to declare too much because I think these people over here could possibly ring Bill Gates and muck it up for me, so I would like a stay for another month or so while I pursue further negotiations."

"You're in negotiations with Bill Gates?" asked the judge with perhaps more incredulity than he intended.

This was too much for me. "Fuck me dead," I muttered to myself. I rose to my feet. "You must be joking?" I exclaimed. "Mr Manly," the judge declared, "you're being disrespectful." No longer intimidated by the judges or the system, I repeated myself, this time pausing between the words for greater emphasis. "You…must…be…joking. The organisers are asking punters to stump up two thousand bucks to hear the great man speak. Why would Bill Gates ever want to meet him? The man can't afford the taxi fare from here to the Opera House and now he's says he's going to have a private meeting with Bill Gates. Oh please."

The judge looked across at the plaintiff. "Mr Lurie?"

"I can't say too much, your Honour, because Manly and Day will do everything to sabotage my meeting with Mr Gates," Lurie replied.

"I'm sure Bill Gates is an astute person who wouldn't be unduly influenced by anyone," the judge remarked. "This is going to happen, is it?"

Lurie grovelled, "Certainly, all I can say is that it looks very promising."

Justice Lawson, who was no fool, had had enough. "I have been in this profession now for some forty years and I've seen people many times do what you are doing, Mr Lurie, and live to regret it. I think that as much as there is hurt and I've got no doubt it's mutual hurt, much as there is enormous antagonism, a deep desire for revenge on your part, you have got to now totally reverse the path you are taking. I believe from the snippets of evidence you have let through here, that you probably have the means to fund this indebtedness, or, alternatively, convince the court that you can make a substantial effort towards so doing in the next week or so. The other course is just going to be a disaster for you." If that wasn't the biggest hint, then I don't know what was. Unbelievably, he was giving Lurie a second chance to cut his losses and run.

Finally, on 7 September 2000, Justice Lawson made an order that the estate of Elliott Elias Lurie be sequestrated and he be made a bankrupt. His Honour also ordered for our costs to be paid out of his estate. Like everything with Lurie, it was always easier said than done. It took four long, arduous years to bankrupt him. Julian and I had to serve Lurie personally every step of the way and then be there in court to see that it all happened.

Hallelujah. We finally had Lurie by the balls. We could go home, rejoice, relax and finally take a breather. It was over. Not long after our success, my wife and I had a barbeque out the back of our house. Our home adjoins a nature reserve and it is quite suited for outdoor entertaining.

Julian and his girlfriend arrived with his mother in tow. Meeting Julian's mother was a revelation and confirmed for me that I had completely misjudged him. She was superb, a delightful, elegant lady and really good fun. When I reminded her of Julian's schoolboy prank taking the clapper off the school bell she added another element to the story which Julian had failed to mention. At the time Julian was expelled, Mrs Day was a governor on the school board. What she found particularly amusing was that not long after that incident she was elected Mayor of Henley-on-Thames. Julian's exploits had made the family famous. Her election slogan had been, "Today's the day to vote Day." What impressed me from talking to Julian's mother was how she enjoyed being involved in community activities. Obviously, this had rubbed off on Julian. He and Ricki were planning another charity walk along the coast of NSW.

Ricki was a tea drinker and I recall that at one point during our barbeque she showed me the tea leaves in her cup. "See this," she said enigmatically, "the curse has been broken. Lurie is gone from our lives."

Desperate for any sign of hope I asked, "You can do this? Read tea leaves?"

"Oh yes," said Ricki with pride, "one of my many skills."

The really frightening part about this nonsense was that we were taking it seriously.

"He will be gone from our lives for good," Ricki predicted. We were so thrilled about this we toasted her prophecy. As you may have guessed, Lurie was still very much part of our lives twelve months later, but Ricki had moved on. Maybe the tea leaves were right — Lurie was out of her life, but so was Julian.

One of our friends, Brendon Woodley, was the local Member of Parliament. He asked how the case was going and as I turned the sausages I replied, "Well, we have made Lurie a bankrupt. It took nearly four years, but it is now done."

"You know," said Woodley, "once a person has been made bankrupt they can't start another court case."

"That was the plan," I admitted.

"The good thing," Brendon added, "looking at the big picture, because I know you have been through real hell, but the good thing is that at least this guy…what's his name?"

"Lurie."

"Yes, well at least Lurie wasn't violent."

"Wasn't violent?" I replied. "The guy assaulted me."

Woodley was dumbfounded. He felt like a fool. In some way, being a Member of Parliament as well as a lawyer, he was part of the system where laws have been dumbed down so much in the criminal's favour. I could never understand how it was that we were relentlessly pursued and sued by Lurie and yet he was always seen by the courts as the victim. He always presented himself as the casualty of the system. It was his magic strategy. If he was pushed by a judge to comply with a deadline he'd claim he needed more time and they always seemed happy to give him what he wanted.

CHAPTER TWENTY-TWO

AVA

By this stage I was seriously broke. My world was coming apart and I was even starting to lose faith in myself. Every week or so I still fronted up to court to catch up with my beloved friend, Elliott Lurie. The more I talked about the case, the more I alienated people and the more they were convinced that I was the sort of person to get myself into trouble anyway. Without prompting from me, women who listened to my tale of woe would often say, "How did your marriage ever survive?" I have no doubt that Jennifer nursed an inner rage at what was going on, but knew instinctively that if she gave voice to that, it would only make matters worse and we'd end up tearing each other apart. At least I was able to vent my feelings with Julian. Wisely, Jennifer became the stoic one in our partnership and that could not have been easy. She has this tremendous resilience and a fierce loyalty. She would stick through thick and thin. Without her there I don't doubt I would have done something reckless.

During these desperate days, I still clung to the forlorn hope that somehow I could start my own business and make a success of my life, if only I knew what it was and if only I could find someone to back me. I'm sure half the world thinks like this. "If only someone out there would give me a go" we all complain in vain.

While I was wasting my time on the worm farm and distracted with the nematode project, I did a lot of research on investment opportunities for a whole range of businesses including olive plantations, emu and ostrich farms, and things like paulownia trees. I cruised around looking at various businesses for sale and at one point ended up checking out a farm in the Hunter Valley. It was a piggery and I didn't need directions to find it. You could smell the stench from a couple of kilometres away. Before long I was standing ankle deep in mud in someone's filthy pigsty. The pig farmer was a nice enough fellow, but even someone as insensitive as me knew that my marriage, which had survived years of pressure because of Lurie's litigation, could not survive a piggery. Although Jennifer had the patience of a saint and had by now endured years of drama in the courts she was not ever going to go for the pigs, no matter how promising the profits might be.

My new-found farmer friend invited me in for a cup of tea. We started chatting and before long I had dumped on him all the travails of my years in the wilderness chasing lost investment opportunities. In a throwaway comment the pig farmer mentioned that he thought education was the best investment there was. In that moment I realised I had been like a dog chasing its tail. My non-compete period was over and running the college had been the best thing I ever did. Into my head popped a single word, 'Ava'.

I first met Ava when I was on the national body of the owners of private colleges. She was perhaps the most fascinating person I'd ever met. A Eurasian lady, her birth name was Ava Mackay, and she was born in Ipoh, Malaysia to a wealthy Scottish tin miner who'd taken a Chinese wife. When World War II came along, Ava was put on a train and sent to Thailand while her father was taken off to a prisoner of war camp. Ava's family weren't in Thailand all that long before the Japanese invaded so she was shipped off to Switzerland where she attended a girls' school for the rest of the war.

When the war was over, the tin mines were close to exhaustion, but the family still had residual wealth and sent Ava to school in Australia. She was a student at a private school in North Sydney where she topped the state in Latin and was accepted into Sydney University to study medicine. While there she met and married this very wealthy Thai playboy who was also doing medicine. They both dropped out of medicine and went back to Thailand where Ava became the number one daughter of her husband's Thai family. That family happened to be the largest owner of agricultural products in Thailand, although their empire was old technology: mining and such. Basically, her father-in-law knew his son was a waster and so he decided to build the next generation using his new daughter. In many Asian cultures there's no word or concept for 'in-law'; if you marry into that family you become part of it.

The father worked Ava day and night and taught her everything. Then he concluded that the next thing that was going to hit Thailand was an automotive industry. He sent Ava to Japan, to learn Japanese and then to bring a car company back to Thailand. So she went to Japan and persuaded Nissan to go to Thailand in partnership with her father-in-law - the company was known as Thai Nissan. The family prospered as a result and they had car dealerships everywhere. As the father had always promised he would do something for Ava she said, "I want you to set up a bank for me." She could see from her experience with the car business that the real money was not in building the cars, but financing their purchase. He set up a bank for her. As you do. Ava built that into the biggest finance company in Thailand.

Then the father made a terrible mistake. He was getting older. The family was exotically wealthy, thanks largely to Ava's efforts and so the father announced that he was handing over control to his number one daughter. He fully endorsed and empowered her, but this was a huge mistake politically. The rest of the family united against her and she was effectively thrown out of the family. She divorced the son and made a deal with the father regarding the children from the marriage keeping their father's Thai name. He let her keep some appropriate assets. After that Ava migrated to Australia with her new husband, who was also a waster and a gambler, and set up a college for international students.

When I met Ava she would have been in her late fifties yet she was still strikingly attractive. I recall seeing some photographs of her when she was young and she looked amazing. She was only about five foot two inches tall, with an attractive figure and this classically beautiful Eurasian face. Ava was always immaculately dressed and invariably wore high stiletto heels. Her appearance was completely deceptive because this petite, dainty-looking woman was tough. I once walked with her from 302 Pitt Street all the way to Circular Quay and even though she was in stilettos I had trouble keeping up. When we arrived I was a wet wreck and she wasn't even puffing.

Recalling Ava's interest in education, I summoned up the courage to contact her. Ava lived in a mansion in Mosman. It was a magnificent place. It had double doors nine feet high. I drove up to the big gates where there was a security camera. Such cameras were fairly rare back then. This camera seemed to zoom in on you. When you hit the buzzer you had to look up and into the camera; otherwise she wouldn't let you in. I buzzed and looked into the camera and, in a very cold and cultivated manner, Ava said, "Oh, welcome. Would you pick up the Fin Review on your way?" When I walked inside the house carrying her newspaper, I noticed that all the Fin Reviews were still in their wrappers. Later, she admitted to me that she only subscribed to the *Australian Financial Review* so the neighbours would see it. Actually, she found the newspaper very boring, but she wanted her neighbours to know she was a serious business person.

At the time I called on Ava, the hottest thing in education was distance learning. Investors were pouring money into the concept. IBM was into it. Microsoft was into it. A local crowd called 'Study World' had raised sixty million dollars to invest in distance learning. Everyone was convinced this was where there was money to be made. With this in mind and not being terribly original, I went to Ava and said, "I have this great idea. How about investing in distance learning?" My pitch was that IBM and Microsoft were doing this and also mentioned Study World's recent cash raising. By this time I had her attention and she was totally focussed. I explained that I needed some seed capital and as I didn't happen to have any, I thought she might be interested in becoming a cornerstone investor.

Suggesting that I didn't have the seed capital was putting it mildly. In fact, the clock was ticking pretty loudly on our personal finances. Jennifer had worked it out that we were about six weeks away from being irrecoverably in default with the mortgage. Ratso was under a bit of pressure. The situation was that in order to survive and get this off the ground, I had to get $160,000 out of Ava for seed capital. I needed that money to be able to put out a prospectus to bring other investors in. Out of that it wouldn't be hard to pay myself a wage of $1,000 a week or so. That would keep the wolves from the door. I put all this together and made my pitch to Ava. Incredibly, on nothing more than a handshake, she gave me $200,000. You don't meet people like Ava every day.

Then she came up with this hair-brained idea. Her suggestion was that to make some serious money out of this, we needed to go upmarket and bring in some prestigious academics. In fact, she knew a recently retired professor who would be ideal. My response was that academics of that calibre wouldn't come anywhere near us. “Not so,” Ava snapped. “These guys love money, Alan. All academics do. They just pretend it doesn’t matter.”

In almost no time, Ava arranged a meeting with this recently retired professor at her house. The opulence was incredible. Apart from the magnificent antique furniture there were sculptures on pedestals and original French Impressionist paintings embedded into the walls with their own little lighting systems. The old academic fitted in very nicely whereas I had to put on a brave face. After some facile discussion about education’s importance to the betterment of mankind, the professor effortlessly slipped in the remark, “And then of course, there would be my fee.” The best salesman on Earth could not have done better. My head started spinning trying to imagine how our little start-up enterprise would ever afford such a fee. “Oh,” Ava shot back, not missing a beat, “you would really have to talk to Alan about that, but it would have to be within the range of this project’s capabilities.” As smooth as silk she started setting expectations that were less than his immediate needs, but something he could obviously live with. She was brilliant with numbers and suddenly here was our recently retired professor positively beaming. There was a bit of chat about the proposed college being a ‘high quality’ affair and that was it.

As the professor disappeared up the driveway, Ava turned to me and said as cold as ice, “Alan, you know the difference between him and us?” As I didn’t feel like I was anything like her or anything like him I didn’t know what to say. “I don't know," I responded helplessly. Waving to our new-found recruit she said, "He could never kill a cat." Confirming her own assessment, she repeated herself. "He could never kill a cat."

This was an incredible thing to say. No Asian would ever kill a cat, not if they were a nice person. Cats are regarded more than just very cute and friendly little characters in Asia. The Chinese and Japanese have the tradition of the 'beckoning cat', or Maneki Neko, a bobtail cat who is deemed wise and lucky. This delightfully elegant Eurasian lady who was rolling in money concluded both of us could kill a cat if that was what was required. How well she understood me. Ratso could kill a cat for sure. Don't worry about killing cats; eliminating the occasional human who stood in her way Ava would have done in her stride.

Ava was an absolute treasure. She thought she could read a person's face like a book and when she met someone she studied their face more than she listened to what they had to say. Westerners are the opposite. They mull over every word you say and yet sometimes have difficulty putting a face to the name. The shape of a person's face was very important to Ava. One potential investor happened to have a square-shaped face which set off alarms bells for her. This was the other side of Ava which made me cringe. Obviously, I couldn't tell this fellow his offer had been declined because his jaw was too square. What most people could not imagine is that someone like me would know quite a bit about Asian culture. That became important in my business dealings with Ava.

ONE ONE FIVE

We put together a team of professors and registered our company, the Australian College of Education. Ava had this most delightful car, a V12 Daimler, which she drove at just short of the speed of sound. I waited for her on the footpath in Chatswood outside the Westpac Bank. We had to open a bank account for the new business and I was there with all our company documents. Ava vroomed up the street and then joined me. With Ava being Asian I knew it had to be all very ceremonial. We took our place in the queue and waited. Eventually, we were shunted off to one side and sat down in front of this absolutely beautiful girl who was either Asian or Eurasian. She started going through the rigmarole, "Yes Mr Manly, yes Miss Mackay, may I borrow your passport to photocopy it? Thank you very much. I'll bring it straight back." The girl accepted Ava's passport with both hands and disappeared. It was theatre and it was beautiful. I knew this girl understood how to play the Asian game. As I already had an account with the bank, they didn't need my passport. Documents were prepared and printed off which we signed. "Right," said the girl from the bank, "we'll now need some funds to open the account."

Somehow, I'd forgotten all about that. "Funds?" I ask. "What's the minimum?"

"Oh," she said, "one dollar."

I took my wallet out and there was this sad, solitary, moth-eaten five dollar note. "Make it five," I announced. I swear it was the last five dollars I had in the world.

"No worries. Would you like me to give you the four dollars back?" the girl from the bank enquired.

"Don't worry about it," John D. Rockefeller replied magnanimously.

We opened our corporate bank account with five dollars. Naturally, I was pretty happy about this. It was all happening, but then I noticed that Ava's face was like thunder. "What could have gone wrong?" I wondered. This account opening business was conducted flawlessly: so Asian, so ceremonial, so theatrical — it was even better than Asia. As we walked out Ava strutted along on her four inch heels, clip-clopping along the pavement heading towards the Daimler. Finally, she could contain herself no longer and turned to me, "Oh, this just makes me so enraged!"
"What?" I asked helplessly.
"Alan Manly opens a bank account and is treated like a king. Five dollars is all he's got! Five dollars! I have half a million dollars at call in the bank and they treat me like shit." The Daimler's tyres were screeching as she took off down the road.

Without Ava there would have been no business and she was not unaware of this fact. When I had drawn up my business plan, I had miscalculated how much money we needed. We were horrendously underfunded. Ava chipped in another $1.3 million. She owned the business, but we made a contract where I would over time pay her back and have an ownership stake. The Australian College of Education opened its doors.

CHAPTER TWENTY-THREE

SEQUESTRATION

It had been a damned sight easier securing an assault conviction than it was branding Lurie a bankrupt. Five days after Justice Lawson made the sequestration order, that is, ordering that the debtor's assets be seized, the wretch applied to Justice Stanshall for a stay of proceedings.

Julian and I met up at Carruthers Café. He had some surprising news. "The other night," Julian explained, "I went down to my local, just for a drink and a chat. The pub is actually split, right? There's a middle area where they serve, and a bar this side and a bar the other side. I sat down and while I was waiting to order I looked across and there was Lurie."

"You are kidding."

"With a woman."

"No," I say incredulously. "And what was she like?"

"Quite attractive, really."

By this stage the mere mention of the name Lurie made Julian and me feel sick. We couldn't imagine anyone actually liking him, much less dating him. "You're sure she just wasn't some random stranger standing next to him at the bar?" I asked.

"They weren't all over each other or anything like that,"

Julian explained, "but they were definitely a couple. He looked quite flamboyant."

"You're kidding. Are you sure it was him?" I asked.

"Oh, it was him all right."

"What happened? Did he see you?"

"Yes," Julian went on, "he looked across and the smile soon vanished from his face. He stared at me and I stared back. By the time my drink arrived he and his lady friend had gone. Completely ruined my night, of course. It's one thing tolerating that bastard in a courtroom, but meeting him in a social situation and in my local is just beyond the pale."

It was like a glimpse into the window of Lurie's life. Occasionally, we heard rumours: that he had a girlfriend with a child on the way, or that he had started legal action against his local council. These things were like words which blew in on the breeze never to be heard again. The only certain thing we knew was that he had a penchant for boarding houses. Why would anyone purporting to be a successful businessman live in such a place? I think it's fair to say that most Australians believe that boarding houses are the last refuge of alcoholics, the homeless, and the friendless. He was definitely that. During the years that we fought this man he never once appeared with anyone by his side, or even with someone as a court supporter. Either Lurie was the quintessential loner, or he led a double life. Whereas we had earlier on a team of lawyers and later friends dropping in from time to time to give us moral support, Lurie had no one.

ONE ONE FIVE

In some circumstances, a person in Lurie's position could be admired for their courage, fighting on alone with no financial backing against a terrible injustice. This was never the case. He had this incredible, instinctive ability to irritate anyone he came into contact with. Time and time again, we would watch the facial expressions of new chums on the bench hearing one of our many legal actions for the first time. Their faces would slowly fall, then harden, then twitch as Lurie effortlessly aggravated them with his shonky legal arguments. For two years running we missed out on watching the Melbourne Cup because Lurie either couldn't take a hint, or couldn't care less. As the time of the race drew closer the judge looked at his watch noticeably and was about to announce a brief adjournment, but Lurie banged on about some obscure, inconsequential aspect of the case completely oblivious to the desire of every other person in the courtroom to watch the race. The race that stops the nation couldn't stop Lurie. It occurred to me that had he been as friendly and convivial as Julian, things might have turned out differently. But this was not to be. He was a completely charmless character without a shred of civility. This was why when Julian saw him in a bar and with a woman, we were totally shocked.

Many a time Julian and I stood around in courtroom corridors bored stiff waiting for our case to be heard. There's only so much you can do with a newspaper once you've read it from cover to cover and done all the puzzles and crosswords. We were desperate to amuse ourselves. At one point Julian floated the idea that our court case would make a great movie. It was to my mind already a movie of sorts in that we seemed to be locked in an episode of the Road Runner/Coyote cartoon every damned day. Credibility was an issue, of course. It couldn't be done as a documentary. No one would believe this story. "What genre, then?" Julian wondered.

"Horror," was my immediate reply. "Lurie in the role of Count Dracula. What proof do we have that he is in fact human?"

Julian replied, "He walks, he talks, he breathes."

"Any vampire can do that."

"And I did see him in a bar with a woman."

Half-joking I said to Julian, "Is she still with us? He really is one of the undead. We should start wearing crucifixes and carrying knobs of garlic. I dare you to touch him. Go on. When we go in, pretend you're picking up a document and just accidentally touch his hand."

Julian shuddered at the thought. "This is ridiculous," he said.

"Of course, it's ridiculous. The whole thing's crazy."

As the bailiff called us in Julian turned and quipped, "I think Daniel Craig would be perfectly cast as me, don't you agree?"

"Who the hell is Daniel Craig?" I asked, exposing Ratso's knowledge of the Arts.

"James Bond."

"Oh. Really?"

We were before Justice Stanshall. Lurie now wanted a stay so as to enable him to raise funds to pay us the debt upon which the bankruptcy petition was based. Justice Stanshall concluded this was not a proper basis to found a stay and described Lurie's evidence as confusing and unconvincing. The application for a stay was lost. However, Lurie appealed that ruling, but when we soon found ourselves back before another judge, he wasn't ready to proceed.

Even though he'd had a month to prepare for this day, Lurie asked the court for more time. When the judge put it to him he acknowledged that the documents had been served on him, but he had not found the time to prepare his response. He informed the judge that he was an extremely busy man. Even someone as pliable as the judge found this hard to believe. "You're busy?" said the judge with more than a note of incredulity in his voice.

"Yeah," replied Lurie, "I'm a very busy man."

"Really? What have you been doing?"

"Oh," said Lurie, and then after a pause while he searched for a suitable lie, but none sprung to mind, he continued, "Oh, just big things, big things, your Honour."

The judge was happy with that. "Oh big things, well that's fair enough. You have been doing big things. Yes, in that case you will need more time, Mr Lurie. Case adjourned."

I sprang to attention. "This is preposterous. My colleague and I have gone to a lot of trouble and spent a considerable amount of time preparing for today. He should be made to present his case now."

"Mr Lurie has explained his circumstances," the judge replied.

"What sort of excuse was that? It's pathetic. You think Mr

Day and I haven't been busy? Do you think we haven't got anything better to do with our lives? But we are here, we are prepared and we don't want to come back here ever again."

"Please, Mr Manly, control yourself. None of your preparation will be wasted."

"Your Honour," I went on, "this situation is oppressive. Mr Day and I do not enjoy coming here."

Julian, ever the peacemaker chipped in, "Much as your Honour's courtroom is a pleasure to be in."

"Thank you, Mr Day."

"The thing is," I complained, "we have wives and children and family to look after and careers to pursue, but we cannot get on with our lives while we have this albatross around our necks. You know, we would actually have had more freedom, if we were out on bail."

The judge put his head in his hands, considered this fairly interesting concept and agreed. "Indeed, I believe you probably would."

"Your Honour, what has happened to Mr Day and me is effectively open detention, as if we were under house arrest."

"You know, I think you are taking this too personally, Mr Manly."

That just brought my bubbling Irish blood to the boil. There was no stopping me now. "How can someone, who has no assets or money, be allowed to unremittingly haul people before the courts on grounds entirely without merit? What if he loses? Doesn't this just become a complete travesty?" I asked. "We didn't initiate legal action. We weren't convicted of fraud. We didn't hurl someone down a flight of stairs. Both Mr Day and I have experienced acute financial hardship as a result of this case, but we have satisfied our creditors. We weren't declared bankrupt and so I say to your Honour, where is the justice in all this? We are innocent men who want to get on with their lives."

"I hear where you're coming from, Mr Manly," said the judge. "We are adjourned."

The good man could not reach a conclusion because what if, after all, the plaintiff was innocent? What if his conviction for fraud had been a miscarriage of justice? What if he had innocently hurled me down a flight of stairs? What if he had been erroneously declared a bankrupt? What if amid the rough and tumble of this cruel, heartless world, Lurie were innocent?

When I cast a glance over at Lurie I looked for some sign. Regret would be too much to hope for, but some sense of regret. Instead, there was no expression on his face at all. He packed up his things with a dull and bloodless look on his face. If one day they found his body chopped into five hundred pieces and dumped in a rubbish bin outside his vile boarding house I would definitely be the first person that the police would have to interview.

Julian and I found ourselves back at Carruthers Café where the mood was one of despondency. We sat there in silence sipping our coffees. "If he were to have an unfortunate accident, I would sleep like a baby," I said. Julian said nothing at all. "He's destroying our lives. We're going to be sitting in this fucking café for the next twenty years because even when he loses he wins. Heaven help us if he ever fucking won." Still nothing from my chubby friend. I looked around the café. Because of its proximity to the courts everywhere you looked there were lawyers and barristers and even police. Perhaps it was not the best place to be discussing the demise of one Elliott Lurie. I really was at the end of my tether. We had tried the proper way, the legal way, and that was a sick joke. In the last few days I had given this a fair bit of thought and was now convinced it was the only way out of this nightmare.

"No, no," said Julian in his classic deadpan style.
"Well then," I hinted to Julian, "the less you know from here on in the better."
"No, no, no," Julian went on. "I mean not you. Let's hire someone. A hit man."
"A hit man?" I said incredulously.
"Yes, a professional hit man. That way there's no come back on us."
"Good God," I said, "we could even choose how it's done."
"What about flattened by a semi-trailer?"
"Or electrocuted in the bath?"
"Thrown off the Gap."
"Burned at the stake on the front steps of the Supreme Court."
After we stopped laughing I said, "A hit man? Really?"
"I could ask around," said Julian with a grin on his face.

Justice Stanshall stayed the proceedings under the sequestration order until 5 October. Justice Lloyd extended the motion until 27 October when Justices Rosen, Lloyd and Robertson in the Federal Court of Australia granted Lurie leave to appeal. Before the Full Bench of the Federal Court on 24 November, Lurie appealed against the sequestration order with an allegation of apparent bias by Justice Lawson. The Full Bench found Justice Lawson's findings soundly based and dismissed the appeal.

On 24 November, Lurie filed an application for special leave to appeal in the High Court of Australia. Pending that application, he sought a stay from Justice Gill in the Federal Court on 1 December. Gill refused Lurie's application for a stay pending the special leave application in the High Court, but stayed the sequestration order for sufficient time to enable Lurie to make any application he wished to pursue before the High Court.

CHAPTER TWENTY-FOUR

THE HIGH COURT OF AUSTRALIA

Any lawyer, even a bush lawyer, will tell you that it is almost impossible to get a case before the High Court of Australia. It concerns itself primarily with constitutional issues, or matters deemed to be in the public interest. Every lawyer we consulted told us the same thing: this case will never get before the High Court; it simply won't happen. Needless to say, Lurie submitted an application appealing his bankruptcy in the High Court. Even more remarkably, it was handwritten. An infuriated Jennifer complained to me, "If Lurie wiped his arse with a piece of paper those idiots would file it."

His application was accepted by the court as apparently his bankruptcy was under a Federal Act which could have something to do with the constitution. It was the same experience all over again. They couldn't get the stamp out quick enough. Never lose a customer. For me to employ a barrister at the High Court would cost a lot of money. Not only that, I knew that even if I won, Lurie wouldn't be able to pay my costs. By now Julian and I had represented ourselves in every court in the country. The High Court wasn't going to faze us one bit.

ONE ONE FIVE

Who would have thought that a fraudulent invoice for $115 would result in both parties appearing before the High Court of Australia over seven years later? Bright and early on Monday morning, 18 December 2000, Lurie's High Court application to stay the proceedings of the sequestration order was heard before a single judge, Justice Gummow in the Law Courts Building in Queens Square, Sydney.

Lurie started by explaining that he was seeking an order for a stay of proceedings pending the hearing of the leave to appeal. He claimed the Full Court of the Federal Court had fallen into error on three counts: that we, the respondents, had deliberately delayed filing documents so that he could not comply with the rules for an appeal; that Registrar Segal had given him the wrong likely appeal date; and that he had been denied natural justice.

Gummow was clearly no fool. "Justice Gill has dealt with your three points already, has he not?"
"Yes, he did, your Honour," Lurie replied.
"Now, if any continuation of the stay were to be granted here, Mr Lurie, you would have to be ready here for a special leave application to be heard as soon as 20 February."
"Yes, Your Honour."

The judge looked around the courtroom. "Is there a lot of other litigation behind this bankruptcy matter?" Gummow enquired. Surely the understatement of the year.
"Yes, there is, your Honour," grovelled Lurie.
"What is the current state of that?"

"Your Honour, the defamation matter against Mr Manly, 13248K/2000, is still in progress."
"Which court?" Gummow wanted to know.
"In the Supreme Court of New South Wales. The other matter is a defamation matter against Julian Day over an email he sent in 1998. There was a hearing before the Court of Appeal last week and…"
"What was the decision in that case?" Gummow asked.
"The Court decided that my appeal would not be heard, but I informed the court that I would be appealing against that."
Gummow sighed. "Dear me," he exclaimed. "Where shall we start?"

"There's more," Lurie said. "I have another case against Mr Day and Mr Manly for preventing me from earning a living over the last seven years by improper motive and defamation."
"Yes, all right," said Gummow. "Now, what do you say, Mr Manly, as to getting this matter disposed of in this court on 20 February?"

Finally, it was my turn to pipe up. "I don't understand why I'm even here."
"That was not the question."
I ignored him and pushed my point. "My colleague, Julian Day, and I have been to over one hundred and eighty hearings. This particular bankruptcy matter has appeared before six Federal Court judges, three individually as well as three sittings of the Full Bench. We've never lost a single hearing and yet here we are again."

"Mr Manly," Gummow added, "the first day on which this court could deal with this special leave application is 20 February 2001."

"I have no objection to a prompt hearing," I replied, "wanting finality after seven years of litigation. But I would have thought that Justice Gill gave Lurie ample time when he gave him twenty-one days to be ready and from what I can understand, Mr Lurie is now saying he wants it deferred. I do not understand why."

I thought I detected a look of sympathy from Gummow. "Look, I understand there is a great deal of animosity between the parties."

"Animosity?" I repeated looking at the detestable piece of shit at the bar table beside me. "I think that's a bit strong," I lied. I was beginning to enjoy myself. "I will be here whenever it suits your Honour, but I shall be seeking some relief in costs."

"That will be decided on 20 February." Gummow replied.

"Well, I would seek a surety of costs, Your Honour, because it is absolutely apparent Mr Lurie is bankrupt."

"I am not entering into that debate. You'll have to take it to the Executive Government."

"Isn't that unfair to me?" I asked.

Gummow wasn't having any of it. He swung back in his chair at the end of it and I saw on his face that he couldn't care less what happened. The stay granted by Justice Gill in the Federal Court was extended up to and including Tuesday, 20 February 2001.

Like many Australians I loved the movie, *The Castle*. This is the story of a typical Aussie battler, a tow-truck driver from memory, who takes on the authorities when he discovers his home has been appropriated by the government. He hires his suburban solicitor who, in a hilarious appearance before the High Court, argues that the government decision was wrong because of "the vibe". When we arrived for our second hearing before the High Court I was sorely tempted to get to my feet and say to the judges, "It's the vibe, your Honour, the vibe." Like the character in that movie, I knew instinctively that I was innocent, and that any fool could see that. It took many years for me to realise that I was the fool in this drama, the fool who believes in logic, and rational and reasonable argument. Julian and I motivated each other by saying, "This surely must be the end." The High Court is the end of the legal road. At least come the end of the day, it will all be over.

Walking into the High Court was seriously different from every other court appearance we had made. The atmosphere was very grave and I felt like I was at the very spring from which the law came. Amazingly, they have traffic lights in the court. When it goes green you can speak. An amber light means you have only a few minutes left and when it goes red you have to sit down and shut up. In front of the judges, there is an army of judges' associates who move up and down and around the place distributing documents from the bar up to the bench and back again. Although there are seven Justices on the High Court, a full bench of the court can be two or more judges. In our case there were two: Justices McHugh and Callinan. For any self-respecting lawyer, this is the pinnacle of their career. This is one place where it is considered absolute sacrilege to arrive without a lawyer. It was hard to miss the disdain on the Justices' wrinkly faces when they learned, horror of horrors, there were not one, but two self-represented parties.

McHUGH J: Mr Lurie. You understand that you have twenty minutes to put your submission.

MR LURIE: I do, your Honour.

McHUGH J: A light will come on when you have about three minutes left.

MR LURIE: Thank you, your Honour. I seek leave to appeal to the High Court because it is the only court empowered to review the administration process.

McHUGH J: That is incorrect. The Court decides cases between parties. It is not an ombudsman, it is not here to rectify general rights and wrongs, nor to investigate people's grievances. It will only grant leave when there is some special point, or that there is a fundamental miscarriage of justice.

MR LURIE: In my submission I detailed a number of issues in the public interest in this matter.

McHUGH J: But, Mr Lurie, they seem to have nothing whatsoever to do with the grounds of judgment and rely on your assertions from the Bar table.

MR LURIE: No, your Honour. The abuse of process in the Federal Court is not an isolated case.

McHUGH J: Where was the evidence in support of this issue in the Federal Court? There is only a judgment which deals with your appeal against Justice Lawson's order.

MR LURIE: Your Honour, if I could summarise the issues. The first issue was that the respondents did not attend the first meeting...

McHUGH J: Mr Lurie, did you make an application in court and was a judgment given in respect of your application?

MR LURIE: Your Honour, this is why I am appealing here…

McHUGH J: No. That is why you cannot appeal here, because you can only appeal against orders of the Federal Court.

MR LURIE: Well, if I may continue, your Honour. I spoke with Chantelle at the Federal Court this morning, at eleven o'clock, and she said normally ...

McHUGH J: Now you are giving evidence from the Bar table.

MR LURIE: Your Honour, I am just verifying that...

McHUGH J: No, you are giving evidence from the Bar table and in this Court we do not admit new evidence.

MR LURIE: Your Honour, I am not seeking to admit new evidence.

McHUGH J: It is new evidence. You are making statements from the Bar table, Mr Lurie, and you want to rely on it. The proper procedure is that you should have made an application to the justices in open court. You relied on a number of matters and Justice Lawson rejected all of them. What is the point of referring them to this Court?

MR LURIE: Because, your Honour, I was not allowed time to prepare the authorities. This is why I appealed Justice Lawson's decision as under rule 52.2(b) there were other sufficient causes.

McHUGH J: Yes, they were listed in your affidavit. You listed four matters: Debtor insolvent; Supreme Court action against the second applicant; High Court application against cost claim; defamation action District Court, first applicant, creditor. An issue was tendered before Justice Lawson. He ruled on it and you had to show that his discretion was wrongly exercised and you failed to persuade the Full Court that that was so.

MR LURIE: Because, your Honour, I had not actually listed those issues.

McHUGH J: Well, that is not sufficient. You must apply to the justices who are hearing the case for an adjournment.

MR LURIE: But that is why I am appealing to you, your Honour.

McHUGH J: It is not sufficient – we are not here as an ombudsman. Mr Lurie, you have to face reality. You have kept the respondents out of a judgment of $37,715 as well as $6,800 in interest since 1997. You refuse to pay it. You lost your case before the District Court. Your appeal to the Court of Appeal was dismissed and you have brought

> many applications, all of which, it would appear, have been lost. When a bankruptcy notice was served on you, you failed to pay it and you resisted the sequestration order on a number of grounds. They were rejected by Justice Lawson, and his judgment was upheld by the Full Court.

For the first time Justice Callinan spoke. He leaned over the bench, put Lurie in the cross-hairs and said, "Mr Lurie, why don't you just pay your debts?" It was for me the most profound moment after all these wasted years. After appearing before an endless line of judges and magistrates in countless courts, we finally encountered one judge who said it all in one single sentence. Lurie stood there like the proverbial stunned mullet and Callinan repeated it, "Why don't you just pay your debts? You keep on disrupting the respondents' lives and affairs by bringing them to court." That moment is forever etched in my memory. Here was a judge who saw right through the charade of a humble plaintiff seeking justice. There was no recovery for Lurie after that and in fact it only got worse. Justice McHugh ripped into him.

MR LURIE: But there was abuse of process, your Honour. Mr Manly contacted the Commonwealth Bank and at least twenty companies...

McHUGH J: That is not abuse of process because they

write to others. Abuse of process is using the court's process for some improper purpose. The fact is that you had a judgment against you. Your appeal was dismissed by the Court of Appeal of New South Wales and you failed to pay it. Your time is up.

MR LURIE: Alan Manly told my clients in the AIDC I was a convicted fraudster.

McHUGH J: Mr Lurie, you do not understand the concept of "abuse of process". If those statements are right, they may give rise to actions on your part, but that is quite different from an abuse of process. It may be a defamatory statement made of you, that is, to say that you are a convicted fraudster.

MR LURIE: No, that was true. I was convicted because Mr Day and Mr Manly took me to court over a $115 invoice for expenses. That part I am not concerned about, your Honour, because it is true. What I am concerned about is them contacting my business associates before serving me with the bankruptcy notice. The law is supposed to protect people from that.

McHUGH J: The law has certain remedies, but the law also protects people who have got judgments. Your time is up. Would you resume your seat, please, Mr Lurie.

MR LURIE: Thank you, your Honour. It is nice to know you get a fair hearing.

McHUGH J: The Court need not hear you, Mr Day or Mr Manly.

As he uttered those words, "The Court need not hear from you," I looked over to Justice Callinan and detected what I thought was a look which said, "unless you want to." Being there, and having prepared so meticulously I shot a look back which said, "Oh, but I want to." Callinan saw this. The expression on his face seemed to change to a "don't you move a muscle" look. I was left with the distinct feeling one should remain silent. For a brief moment, I was feeling quite hurt. How often is it that anyone, never mind a schmuck like me, ends up before the High Court? "You can't be serious," I thought. "Let me tell you what's been going on here." Fortunately, common sense prevailed and I said nothing. McHugh resumed.

McHUGH J: The applicant seeks special leave to appeal against an order of the Full Court of the Federal Court dismissing his appeal against an order for the sequestration of his estate made on 7 September 2000. The

> sequestration order was made for non-compliance with a bankruptcy notice. That notice arose out of the applicant's failure to comply with a District Court order that he pay the respondents the sum of $37,715-odd and interest thereon, which relevantly amounted to almost $6,800. Nothing relied on in the applicant's argument today would warrant this Court granting special leave to appeal against the order of the Full Court. There is no special leave point in the case. The application is dismissed with costs. It follows that the stay that was granted by Justice Gummow ends.

Oh, the richness of the irony of Lurie claiming to be a victim of abuse of process was not lost on me. He was the master of abuse of process and had played merry hell with our lives by abusing the courts and the justice system. Without having to utter a word, Ratso and the British Bulldog had triumphed.

CHAPTER TWENTY-FIVE

THE DRUMMOYNE SAILING CLUB

Julian and I walked out of the High Court feeling like rock stars. I guess we are too used to watching too many television programs where the victors emerge from the court and are embraced by their families and swamped by tearful well-wishers while a pack of cameramen and photographers capture the moment. When we stepped into the light of day there was nary a soul about. There'd been too many court cases over too many years for any of our friends to make the effort to be there. It wasn't every day that a person represented themselves before the High Court of Australia. Whereas I felt this tremendous surge of adrenalin powering through my system, Julian was his usual deadpan self. He looked like he'd just picked up his dry cleaning. "What now?" he said.

"What now exactly," I replied. "We should celebrate."

"Alan, we've been down this road before."

"This really is the end," I said emphatically. "After the High Court there is nowhere else for him to go."

What better place to celebrate our win than the Drummoyne Sailing Club. The place looked like a nice enough bistro, but inside it was quite noisy. You couldn't hear yourself think. Also, there was a buffet which meant shouting, screaming hordes of people. The good news was there was a restaurant upstairs, called Ecco, which looked more intimate and, of course, more expensive. Reading my mind, Julian let me know quickly and quietly that he was broke, at the moment, and perhaps Ecco was a tad expensive. The thing about Julian is that he's perpetually short of money. "Seeing as it's a special occasion, my shout," I announced magnanimously. Anything to get us out of the hell-hole of the bistro.

The situation was complicated slightly by Julian arriving with not one, but two women on his arm. I was aware he and Ricki split up. Both women hailed from Iceland apparently, and were introduced as 'flatmates'. Julian met them at his local where they had been staying after a stint working down south as fruit pickers. When they complained about the severe shortcomings of their lodgings, Julian offered them the use of a couple of spare sleeping bags. Something was lost in translation and they thought he had offered them somewhere to stay. My guess was that they were settled into his flat for the long term.

They certainly didn't look like fruit pickers. Both were magnificent-looking young women with long blonde hair and they were dressed up to the nines. Even more incongruously, there was mention of them being out here on family reunion visas, but they were easily mid-twenties and there was never any discussion about their supposed relatives. From the glint in Julian's eye I suspected he was in a relationship with one of them, but I couldn't fathom which one.

We were the first diners of the evening and although it was

a bit after six the restaurant was still closed. The maitre d' duly appeared looking a bit wild eyed, even at that time of the night, and we pleaded to be allowed in; anything to escape the thunderdome downstairs. Julian was in his element: beautiful women, convivial company and exquisite food and wine. He enthusiastically recalled a number of reviews he'd read on the place. As their English was not perfect Julian had to interpret occasionally as they read the menu, which he loved.

I was in half a mind to explain to our Icelandic friends that it was not necessary to order everything on the menu. Although they were not big girls, they ate more in one sitting than I would in a week. I wondered if starvation was an issue in their country. Whenever we talked of this outing in years to come, Jennifer and I referred to Julian's flat-mates as 'the Vikings'. Despite this propensity to consume everything, there was drama with the salad, or to be more accurate, the lettuce. It was not warm enough. This was the sort of restaurant where a lettuce leaf is so crisp it is supposed to snap at eighty decibels. The waiter was called over and after some translation from Julian it was decided that they would take the salad back and warm it by the oven for a moment. As I sat there I had a feeling I knew what was going to happen and sure enough when the salad was returned by the waiter, one of the Vikings took one look at it and without even tasting it announced, "Too hot now."

If I thought they could eat like there was no tomorrow, I was completely taken aback by their seemingly endless ability to consume alcohol. Obviously, these girls were costing Julian a bomb in day-to-day living expenses. Once they had a few drinks under their belt, the Vikings became different people and looked on us with complete disdain. In her stilted English one of the Vikings, the one with the tattoos, let it be known that they far preferred Tokyo. They had spent the winter there. "Oh, I've been there," said Jennifer, trying to be civil. "I was in Tokyo for a conference a few years ago." It transpired that they knew Jennifer's hotel and revealed a working knowledge of that establishment which seemed far too familiar for them to have been guests of the place. No doubt they were picking different fruit in Tokyo.

"Not boring there," Viking No. 1 announced.

I couldn't resist. "And I'm sure at this very moment there are people eating at restaurants in Tokyo wishing they were here at the Drummoyne Sailing Club." Julian and I laughed.

"Court case over now, yes?" the other Viking enquired. We all happily nodded.

"Julian and Alan win, yes?"

"That's right," I agreed, surprised that she even seemed interested. "Let me say that I could never have done it without the unfailing support of young Julian."

"Thank you, Alan," said Julian.

"Many times the baton was passed between us. He or I would be fed up or exhausted and the other would take over."

Julian rose to his feet. "I would like to propose a toast. But first let me say that when this all started eight years ago I asked Alan to stand by me, and he did. There were more times than I care to remember when I would have given up - indeed at one point I did give up. But had we done so we would have lost everything. And so I ask you to raise your glasses and toast that hallowed place where from few ever return in triumph. The High Court." We clinked our glasses and repeated the toast.

"How much your prize?" Viking No. 2 wanted to know.
"Prize?" I asked.
Julian chipped in, "She means damages."
"Yes. Julian will take us back to Tokyo."
"No, no, no," said Julian sheepishly.
"Yes. You win. Yes," she enthused. "How much you win?"
I said, "Nothing."

Her face actually fell right there in front of me. The jaw dropped as if she had been king hit. "Our opponent is bankrupt," I explained. "Lurie has no money and so we will get nothing." I guess it was hard for outsiders to comprehend that so much time and effort could go into something for no financial gain. The absurdities of our system of justice were lost on people from the land of fire and ice.

As had happened so many times before, I politely enquired what Julian had been up to, meaning in his non-Lurie world. Had I not known him as well as I did, or at least better than most, I would probably not have pushed it further and read his "Oh, this and that," at face value which normally translates as "Not much, really." However, after one of the Vikings teased him with a "Walking, walking, always walking," I pushed him and in dribs and drabs the most interesting story emerged.

ONE ONE FIVE

His walking adventures had become a big part of his life. By the time of his third walk, this time from Huskisson to Bateman's Bay, people started becoming interested in what Julian was doing. On his fourth walk he stopped overnight at a hotel at Tathra called Froggy's Pub. Trust Julian to find a pub in the middle of nowhere. In the morning a radio station rang the pub to interview him. From there he followed this track along the cliffs through quite heavy scrub. Because he was the first person to walk through there in a long time, he was covered in spiders' webs. And then on to Tuross Beach which is only about three kilometres long, but very tricky. When it rains precipitation runs off the hill at one end and floods the narrow, shaly beach. As a result the sand is quite soggy and hard going. Although it was still about eight in the morning, it was already quite hot.

As he approached the end of the beach, he noticed a couple exercising their dogs. They'd come down to see him and spur him on because they knew this was a really difficult beach. After a bit of a yarn the man said, "When we heard you on the radio we thought you might run out of water." Julian was much relieved as he'd already gone through most of his water because of the heat and the hard slog on that beach. They gave him some cold water and then handed over a cheque for two hundred dollars.

By now people started tracking his route and popping down to say hi. Some would stay with him for a few hours or even a full day. More charities started becoming involved. Julian started honing his idea. Each walk took him along the coastline. In those places where there were cliffs or rocks he couldn't get around, surf life saving clubs, volunteer coastal rescue crews, or even local people offered to pick him up in a boat and take him around to the next beach.

Julian's idea for going for a walk along the coast to clear his head was soon completely unrecognisable. In a few short years it had become 'Waterline', a full-blown charity. The Waterline Foundation has three directors and a management team of about ten people. The entire Australian coastline has been divided up with groups responsible for walking a specific section of beach in their local community to raise money. Each section is monitored by satellite and the participants tracked on Google Maps. In August 2012 it's been estimated that as many as a quarter of a million people will be involved. The goal is to raise many millions of dollars in forty-eight hours. It is such a crazy idea it's brilliant. What better way to raise money for charity than to walk along a beach and enjoy yourself.

I marvelled at the way this completely unprepossessing man, who was genuinely modest and humble, who loathed talking about himself, was able to harness an idea and exploit it, but not for his benefit, but for others. It occurred to me that Julian was the universal opposite of Lurie. Both were involved in the IT industry, both were constantly broke and you just knew from taking one look at either of them that they would go to their graves without a bob to their name. Lurie's reaction to his dire financial circumstances was to try and extort money from others — to make legal threats and create an enormous fuss over nothing — forcing the victims to pay up. Julian never had any money because he was forever giving it away. There was something truly admirable about him. He didn't care about money, just so long as he had enough for a drink at the pub. I certainly wasn't like that. While it was true that I was as hungry for money as the next man, success mattered more to me than anything. I guess I was hot-wired to make something of myself and hoped that financial rewards would flow on in my wake.

We ordered sweets and I lashed out and ordered a De Bortli dessert wine. The Sailing Club was growing on me. By now it was dark and the fairy lights in their beautiful big trees were reflecting off the water. The breeze was coming up the harbour and for the first time in a long time I felt relaxed. Well, at least less manic than the norm. The grog was, of course, kicking in and I was smiling. It did take me back to that afternoon years before when we watched as Julian's underpants floated down from his apartment. Eventually, I noticed the kicks under the table. Jennifer and I said our farewells to Julian and the Vikings and headed home.

As we drove up the driveway of our home I noticed out of the corner of my eye an object sticking out of our letterbox. My wife didn't see it and I said nothing about it. We went to bed, but I could not sleep. Really, I hadn't had a decent night's sleep in over eight years. Through perspiration alone I had destroyed something like a dozen pillows and countless bed sheets. It astonishes me when I meet people who have used the same pillow for twenty years. Mine were destroyed; they disintegrated from exposure to excessive bodily fluids; from nightmares which caused me to sweat like a rat cornered in a sauna. This was another thing Julian and I shared. He once told me he also had managed to completely ruin bed linen through endless night sweats.

I lay awake in bed staring at the ceiling. All I could think about was that thing in the letterbox. I was sure it was an envelope. I stared at the ceiling until I could bear it no more. I couldn't take the risk of Jennifer finding that envelope first. One time when I was in China she had opened one of these government gold envelopes. Our son, James, was standing next to her and asked innocently, "What is that, Mummy?" She read the documents and went into total emotional meltdown. "This fucking thing will never end," she screamed at me on the phone. Later, James made the acute observation that this case had been going on for more than half his life and he was now seventeen.

Down to the letterbox in the dead of night I walked, like a man on death row going to his place of execution. In the torch light I could see that it was the usual government gold envelope. I pulled it out and ripped it open. As I had guessed all along, it was from Lurie. Another summons to appear in the Federal Court this time to defend alleged breaches of the *Trade Practices Act.*

By this time I was in a shocking state. I was tired, hung over, demented. Out on the street it was deadly quiet. Not a sound stirred. No dogs barked, no babies wailed, no cars drove past. My neighbours, all good men and true, were tucked up in their beds. Did this not happen to other people? Who else in this crazy city was standing on their front lawn in their pyjamas at midnight reading legal correspondence from a maniac? My thoughts turned to the good Mr Davidson, the paint man, a resident of a neighbouring suburb, and wondered if I would end up as mad as him. It crossed my mind to start screaming. When the neighbours poked their heads out of their windows I could cry out, "Call the police. A man is being murdered. Me. I'm being murdered." Thankfully, common sense prevailed. Screaming was far too melodramatic for my taste although I would have howled at the moon if it'd do me any good. Instead I sat down on the footpath and wept like a man on the verge of a nervous breakdown. Ratso was cornered and too tired to jump. I felt I had nowhere to go.

CHAPTER TWENTY-SIX

STANDING BEHIND A BANKRUPT

The euphoria of our win in the High Court was short lived. Lurie commenced a new action in the Federal Court claiming we had breached the secondary boycott provisions of the *Trade Practices Act.* Lurie claimed his bankruptcy was 'an instrument of oppression' due to our unconscionable conduct and made an application for the annulment of his bankruptcy. He lodged a Notice of Motion with the ACCC (Australian Competition and Consumer Commission) and applied for an immediate and permanent restraint against us for breaching sections 45D, 45DB, and 51AC of the *Trade Practices Act.* Action was commenced against the AAT (Administrative Appeals Tribunal) over the recent cancellation of his Newstart Allowance and new writs were issued for defamation. His Statement of Claim included damages for loss of immediate income, damage to reputation, loss of income from time spent prosecuting and defending malicious litigation, and loss of income through intellectual property theft.

Things were very bleak when Julian and I met at Carruthers Café. "I've found someone," whispered Julian, "to do the job."
"What job?" I asked.
"Lurie." Then he made a throat cutting gesture.
Having forgotten my earlier outburst, I was confused.

"What?"
"You know, a hit man." Julian explained.
"Oh that."

He'd spoken to a friend of a friend at his local and been put on to some bikies who would knock off Lurie for an agreed fee. "They're surprisingly cheap," said Julian.
"How much?"
"$1,500 was the figure quoted."
"Jesus Christ, Julian. How could it be a professional job for fifteen hundred?"
"That was the price quoted," he said firmly.
"Fifteen hundred. Jesus. About the price of a good suit."
"Well, they started at $15,000 and when I explained I didn't have that kind of money they admitted they were light on for work at the moment and gave me a bit of a discount."
"A bit of a discount? At that price they'll fuck it up for sure," I complained. "Bump off the wrong guy or get caught and blab it all to the cops."
"No," Julian enthused, "they assured me they only use professional hit men."
"Too much can go wrong."
"You realise this could go on for the rest of our lives," Julian warned. "I'm telling you there is no end in sight this way. Legally. We have to get this thing off the legal treadmill."

We finished our coffees and made our way to the Federal Court. It was March 2002. One of the recent innovations made by the court was to make available a communal computer for the general public. If you were one of the parties to a matter, you could use the computer to look up things and access information on your case. It was just a PC with a printer attached. You had to supply your own paper and theoretically were allowed only fifteen minutes per session. Julian started fiddling on the computer while I filed some documents.

The female clerk on duty that day came out carrying a file in which to lodge my documents, but discovered that it was the wrong file. As she was about to take it back the phone rang. She put down the file, took the call, and then hung up. After that she left to get the correct file, but left the other file on the counter. The thing is, these clerks became so used to seeing us around the place, they assumed Julian and I were lawyers. While I was standing there twiddling my thumbs, I noticed this file had the same case number on it as ours did. How curious.

The clerk had left the file on the counter in front of me. Well, not exactly in front of me, but close enough. I looked around. There was no one else there apart from Julian and me. I waited a moment and then Ratso made his move. I pulled the file over and started flipping through the papers. Obviously, it was Lurie's file and knowing the clerk would be back any second I riffled through it looking for something, anything to give us an edge. By this stage, approaching a decade in the courts, I was an absolute master of speed-reading legal phrases, of reading things upside down, of knowing which box on which form was just procedural guff and which was not. I flipped through the file furiously and suddenly there in front of me was an application from Lurie for an exemption from filing fees. The fact that the court had stamped it verified that he had been exempted from paying a fee. The revelation stunned me. Like the proverbial criminal with a smoking gun, I was standing there file wide open and with this document in front of me when the clerk returned.

"What are you doing?" she wanted to know. "Give that back."
"No," I replied emphatically.
"That's not your file," the clerk complained in a dull kind of way.
Completely ignoring her I asked, "This exemption application of Lurie's was granted?"
She extended her right arm, elbow on the desk, palm upwards, like her hand was a receptacle for rubbish, as if by gesture alone she could convince me to stop being childish and return to her possession a single piece of A4 paper.

If Ava had taught me anything it was the importance of reading faces. My young clerk was about twenty-something, a plain girl very heavily made-up. In fact she had so much make-up on, I couldn't read her reaction. But somewhere in those eyes I detected just the slightest hint of panic.
"Come on," she insisted.
"Get lost."
She looked across at Julian, but he was preoccupied with the computer so she gave a small sigh and then left to gather reinforcements.

It occurred to me that Lurie was doubtless making the lives of these clerks a misery as well. I had another look at Lurie's exemption application. It had been filled in by hand and I recognised the spidery handwriting as his. Then I noticed an anomaly on the form. A classic accidental yet deliberate blunder that was pure Lurie. Although the application had been stamped "Approved" the signature box was blank. I couldn't believe what I was seeing. The cunning bastard had applied for an exemption and had it approved even though technically because he hadn't signed the form he hadn't applied at all.

I walked over to Julian and showed him what I had discovered. Julian is extraordinarily intelligent and a dangerous man to put in front of a computer. I'd sometimes seen him fiddling about on this computer and half-suspected that he was playing games to while away the hours. He seemed to take no notice of what I was saying. With a fat, stubby finger pointing at the screen, Julian said, "Look at this." I looked at the screen which showed various columns of numbers. He had gone through the system and somewhere amid thousands and thousands of pages of legal junk, Julian brought up on the screen a section which displayed fees, and more importantly, unpaid fees owing to the court. What we were looking at were the accumulated and unpaid filing fees owed to the court by one Elliott Elias Lurie.

My eyes almost fell out of my head. For us, this was one of the great watershed moments in this case. On the screen in front of us was something we had never known. Lurie owed the Federal Court over $40,000. You cannot begin, or go on, with legal action without filing documents and for that you have to pay a small filing fee. Slowly, but inexorably over the years, Lurie had accrued a debt to the Federal Court of $40,000 in unpaid filing fees. "You know what this means," Julian said angrily. "The Federal Court is financing Lurie's legal expenses." We realised the system was anything but impartial. The man at the bar table opposite us for the past ten years was being funded by the very court we were sitting in. The man who seemed intent on destroying our lives had a sponsor.

By the time the clerk returned with the Registrar of the Federal Court in tow my blood was boiling. The Registrar, a person of considerable authority, looked to me like a self-important, pompous twerp. In front of me the clerk explained to the Registrar how she had accidentally left a confidential file on the bench and that I had 'taken' a document from the file. Mr Registrar politely asked me to hand back Lurie's application, but I was having none of it. Brandishing the form I railed, "You gave him an exemption from paying a filing fee, didn't you?"

"We won't be discussing that, Mr Manly," the Registrar responded crisply.

"And," I continued, "the exemption was given without Lurie even applying for it."

"That's not correct."

"This document is unsigned."

The clerk and the Registrar looked at each other and then at the piece of paper I waved in front of them. "You waived

his filing fee of your own volition."
"Mr Lurie is unemployed," the clerk replied defensively.
"What proof do you have that he's actually unemployed?"
They seemed too stunned to respond. "Have you bastards even checked that he's really on the dole?"
"Control your language, Mr Manly," the Registrar warned. "Now please…"
"You turds have given Lurie a $40,000 line of credit. You're supporting him financially so he can harass us."
"Not so, not so," the Registrar responded dismissively.
"Now I know you're a liar."
"I'm not putting up with this," he moaned. From the half-hearted response I could smell blood in the water. I refused to back down and the argument became more heated. Sheriffs and other Federal Court staff appeared, but I refused to be intimidated. The Registrar accused me of making wild, baseless accusations and threatened there would be extremely serious consequences if I refused to give back the documents I had taken.

"If you don't give the material back I'll ask the Sheriff to intervene."
I dug in my heels. "No."
"We'll take you before a judge. You'll be found in contempt of court and imprisoned."
We all stood there waiting to see what would happen. The situation was on a knife edge, but I was determined to stand my ground. It was then that the Registrar overplayed his hand and waved a red rag at the raging bull before him. "This could all end horribly for you, Mr Manly. You could

end up a bankrupt." The word bankrupt was toxic to me. The irony of that cheap jibe rippled through my mind. "Go for it, buddy," I goaded him.
"Very well," said the Registrar, "You were warned. Sheriff, arrest this man."

No one moved. Certainly not the sheriff standing beside him. Years of hanging around these courts had taught me that these people were loath to do anything, but if I was going down, it would be in a blaze of glory.
"Right, let's go then," I screamed. "Come on. Get your handcuffs out, smart arse. Haul me up before the judge. You think you can threaten me, you pathetic piece of shit. Everyone in this registry office, every person in this court is liable and you have been busted big time. You pricks have destroyed my fucking life. You think you can bankrupt me? I'll have your fucking house before this week is out."

It was terrible. Years of pent up frustration exploded from me. The near albino was glowing like a danger beacon and I was wringing wet with sweat. Had Lurie been unfortunate enough to have walked in at that moment I would have torn him apart limb from limb. I berated them for agreeing to defer payment for filing fees, that by doing so the Federal Court was actually funding Lurie's legal action. What they were doing violated one of the bedrock beliefs of the Common Law. There is a very important and fundamental concept in law that you cannot 'stand behind' a bankrupt. If you do this, if you stand behind a bankrupt, if you loan money to a bankrupt, you become a party to the action and are liable for any losses or costs in the matter.

Lurie was a bankrupt. The Federal Court was loaning him money which meant they were funding his legal action. The court was supplying vendor finance to their customer. This legal reign of terror was being perpetrated by the very court which purported to administer justice fairly and impartially. By funding Lurie they, the Federal Court, were standing behind a bankrupt. An interesting question was how many such actions did they fund themselves?

As I raved on I could see genuine fear in all their faces. They realised they were dealing with a mad man. This was not something to be proud of and totally out of character for me. I am not a bully. I'm actually a funny person. A bit manic, but amusing and this was what I had turned into. Driven to despair by a remorseless litigant, who was unwittingly assisted by the ineptitude of these gormless court administrators. Julian sauntered over and bent down to pick up Lurie's application form which had fallen to the floor during my ranting. He put it on the enquiries desk, turned, picked up my briefcase, put his arm around me and walked me to the door while I was still a free man. "I'll be subpoenaing that document," I cried out to no one in particular.

The events of that day were so frantic with so much adrenalin pumping the whole thing was like a blur in my mind. Whatever I did worked. Things were never the same after that. Whenever I walked into the Federal Court after that, the registry staff were extremely courteous and deferential. To my amazement, I detected an attitude of respect.

CHAPTER TWENTY-SEVEN

BUYING BACK THE FARM

Charles Claymore was dead. Suicide. Apparently. After being done over by Mark Gatehouse, I was paid out, and Claymore went on to set up another college which ultimately failed. Christina, the child bride from Mexico, or was it the Spanish-speaking child bride from Bolivia, told the police that Claymore, who had been suffering severe depression, went to work at his office one Saturday morning. At some stage, Christina went shopping and when she drove past his office she noticed his car was still there. He didn't come home that night, but his child bride didn't go looking for him. In a scene eerily reminiscent of the morning we took him to hospital, Christina made no effort to enquire as to his wellbeing. Cleaners found him on the Sunday. I believe he left a note for his femme fatale. Medical tests established that he had taken an overdose. Poor Charles. Such a strange, complex man. In his day he was brilliant, but life seemed to spiral out of control from that moment the phone he was speaking on was struck by lightning. Like so many things with Charles you didn't know whether it was true or not.

Once the press latched on to this story, there was a near riot from students of the college who worried that with the death of Claymore all their fees paid in advance were in jeopardy. We've all seen these stories in the media — a college goes bust and the students are left high and dry. Colleges are now required to have strictly controlled assurance schemes so this should not happen.

Mark Gatehouse was still alive and kicking, but he may also have been thinking he would be better off dead. After our big split Gatehouse, who had sole control of SBC, made the fatal mistake of becoming involved in the day-to-day management of the college. I had run the college very successfully and I'm sure Gatehouse concluded that if I could do this anyone could. Although he privately acknowledged that I was the one who kept the business going, Mark would posture in front of people that he was the great wizard behind it all. Jennifer was very critical of Mark, claiming that he couldn't run a two-door dunny. He was a software genius preoccupied by his harem of assistants. At times he would come up to me and ask, "What Bluebird have you got for me this year?" The Bluebird being the Bluebird of Happiness which was meant to sit on his shoulder and provide seemingly endless wealth. I said to Mark many times, "Be careful what you wish for. One day the Bluebird will come and crap on your shoulder." In the end, this is what happened, and sadly Gatehouse only succeeded in driving the college business into the ground.

The Statewide Business College at 1841 George Street, Sydney, was placed in administration. There were full page spreads in the Sunday newspapers about the demise of the college which brought shame to Gatehouse and his family.

When this news reached my ears I must confess to feelings of elation. Schadenfreude at its worse, I'm afraid. For me this was the ultimate opportunity to get back what I had poured my heart and soul into all those years ago. I felt that I had created that college and it was rightfully mine. I contacted Ava and told her what had happened. She was interested. Looking me straight in the eye she said, "I'll back you on one condition: that Alan Manly works there full time." "It's a deal," I replied enthusiastically. However, I did warn her they might want half a million dollars.

What has to be remembered is that I used to own this business. I knew every nook and cranny of those accounts and where the bodies were buried. The administrators handed over the company accounts and financial reports and before my eyes was a bigger catastrophe than I could have ever possibly imagined. When I was there we had about 1,500 students, some fifty staff and $1.3 million in the trust account. After a couple of years with Gatehouse at the wheel, the student numbers dropped to seven hundred, the staff numbers soared to a hundred and all the money in the trust account had vanished. The staff hadn't been paid for a month and superannuation money was missing. It seemed like every employee had their own personal assistant. Cars, credit cards, fuel cards, mobile phones and laptops were given to all and sundry. We had ten days to put in an offer.

Out of the blue, I received a phone call from the landlord of 1841 George Street. He remembered me from when I had run the college and had heard on the grapevine I was interested in buying it back. He said the rent was six months in arrears and it transpired that it was his demand for payment which had tipped the business into administration. The landlord was very critical of the former managers and said he would be delighted to have me back along with Ava whom he knew from other business ventures. "Not that I'm an authority or anything," the landlord said, "but if I were you I'd be inclined to offer about $60,000."

"$60,000. For the business?"

"Of course, I wouldn't presume to tell you what to pay for a business."

"No," I agreed.

"No, but if I were you, I think sixty would get you over the line." What a heads-up. Naturally, I passed this tip on to Ava.

On the appointed day, we met with the administrators around the conference table in the boardroom. Naturally, the administrators are trying to secure the best possible price, but it's difficult to play hard ball when everyone knows buyers are thin on the ground. There was a lot of waffle from them and precious little from Ava and me. After some more discussion, Ava looked at the administrators and said, "Would you please excuse us so we can discuss things in private?"

The administrators all shuffled out of their own boardroom and waited out in the corridor like naughty schoolboys while we discussed our offer. Ah, the power of money. I'd never seen such brilliant technique. This was just Ava at play. The administrators knew either factually or instinctively that Ava was rolling in dough. There was really nothing for us to discuss. She just wanted to humble the administrators. She could get away with things like that. If it had been me, I would have left their boardroom and chatted in the corridor. After a suitable period of time had elapsed Ava said, "Call them back in now, Alan."

The administrators filed back in sheepishly and we got down to business. All eyes were on Ava. She was silent. Her face was completely blank. She waited. We all waited. A good minute ticked by. Then, in a voice barely above a whisper, she said, "I'll make one offer, and I'll make it only once. $160,000."

One of the suits paused. "Sorry, Madam," he said, "you have the slightest accent. Would you be kind enough to repeat that?"

"I said, and I won't be saying it again. $160,000. That is my final offer. Take it or leave it."

"It's a deal," exclaimed one of the administrators, perhaps a little too enthusiastically. There was still a bit more bargaining about various issues and Ava was fantastic in creating the theatre. Every time a new element of the deal was put on the table, she insisted they leave the room so we could think about it. When the administrators left the room for a second time, I said to Ava, "About the price. I am sure I said to you that $60,000 would get us there." I worried that I had mumbled the figure and that she had misunderstood me. "Oh yes, Alan," she replied, "but it's so fiddly. This is how you get things done." What she had done was so unpredictable, so very un-Asian. The constant haggling of the Asian drives the Westerner mad. Knowing this I had been expecting this meeting with the administrators to go for days.

The college was ours. Three years after I had been kicked out I bought it back for less than what I was paid out by Gatehouse. It was bitter sweet revenge. The administrator asked me to meet him at 9am sharp on the footpath in front of the college entrance. "We'll then go through everything," he explained reassuringly. This was good news to me as we really had no idea who was who and what was what. Having come across administrators before I was always suspicious that all they ever did was collect their fee and scarper. This guy was different.

On the morning of 22 November, Jennifer and I arrived out the front as instructed at about five minutes to nine. The administrator was already there and his usual charming self. "Good to see you," he said. Instinctively, I moved to enter the college, but he stopped me in my tracks. "Now, I have with me one hundred and twenty copies of this letter I've drafted to hand out to the staff which explains what's happened." The man was organised; you had to give him that. With that he handed over the one hundred and twenty letters and said, "Unfortunately, I have another appointment. I'll leave you in charge." The administrator promptly walked off down the footpath and disappeared never to be seen again.

Despite this unexpected development, we walked back into

the college feeling about ten feet tall. It was an incredible feeling, such an adrenalin rush after the public humiliation of being sent packing. We were back. The college was, of course, in an even bigger mess than we had imagined. The staff gathered in a large classroom, some looked frightened, many in tears. The first thing I needed to do was to get the college teaching. "Those of you who are assigned to a timetable," I announced, "go to your assigned classroom and start teaching." About half those in the room then left. After that we started interviewing everyone. Under the terms of the sale, all the staff were retrenched and those who were needed, re-hired. It was a horrendous experience. People threw their company-supplied mobile phones at me; hurled keys across the room and abused me. There were salaries unpaid and superannuation funds stolen and they vented all their anger with the former owners on me. Then the creditors starting turning up. The cleaners hadn't been paid, the stationery suppliers were desperate for their money, and then two men arrived with a trolley to repossess the toilet paper. "We're here to take our toilet rolls back," they announced.

"How much are you owed?"

"$238."

I explained that we were a different company, that we had bought the assets and not the liabilities, but these guys didn't give a damn about that. They started packing up their cartons of toilet paper. In the end Jennifer offered them a personal cheque for the outstanding amount and we managed to hang on to the toilet paper.

Starting from scratch we restructured the whole college and merged it with our existing business and the Australian College of Education went from one student to six hundred overnight. Not that it was all smooth sailing. We desperately needed more investment. Jennifer worked with me in the business and she was there when my board presentation to the people who would allow us to issue a public prospectus for investment was a complete dud. The chairman of the board was the former federal treasurer, John Kerin, and with him on the board was Professor Tom Valentine, an academic of renown. Just when it looked like all was lost Jennifer charmed them into having another look at our proposal and they soon became ardent supporters of the project. I was not alone in recognising her business acumen. Some years later, Jennifer was nominated for Businesswoman of the Year.

Finally, I saved the money to pay Ava back by taking a miserable salary, working long hours, and travelling to China endlessly to build up the business. At long last, things were going well in my career, but there was still some unfinished business to attend to.

CHAPTER TWENTY-EIGHT

DAY AND MANLY -V- THE FEDERAL COURT

It is considered a fundamental right that every citizen has access to the courts. If, however, you abuse that right and institute legal proceedings to harass people without reasonable grounds you could be declared a vexatious litigant. Taking away a person's right to legal redress is considered pretty drastic and never done lightly, quickly, or in fact, much at all. Since the colony of New South Wales was founded in 1788 there have been only two people declared vexatious litigants: Michael Edward Spartz (1990) and Raymond Stanley West (1992). Not surprisingly, having someone declared a vexatious litigant can only be done through the courts. To have Lurie declared a vexatious litigant would be a process which would wind its way through the courts for another five to seven years. If Julian and I did this we were looking at a fifteen to seventeen year battle.

We were back in the Federal Court, this time before Judge Snarl. I can't remember his actual name, so Snarl will do. Such was his demeanour he looked like he'd just been delivered to the court in an ambulance after being hospitalised overnight for ingesting arsenic. Julian wasn't there and Lurie

was a no-show. The bailiff called, "Next case."
Justice Snarl roared, "Where are they? Where are they?" meaning, where are the lawyers. "There are none," said the bailiff.
"None, what do you mean, none?" the judge demanded to know.
The bailiff said meekly, "They're appearing in person, your Honour." The judge looked at me in sheer horror and announced, "Not interested. Not having litigants in person." As I knew I was perfectly within my rights to be there, I just remained where I was and kept my mouth shut. Do the Asian thing, use the silence.

After a suitable pause Judge Snarl asked, "Righto — who's here?"
"I'm here."
"And who do you represent?" the judge asked.
"I represent the defence."
"Where's the other guy?"
"The other guy? You mean my colleague?"
"No. The plaintiff. Where is he?"
"I don't know," I replied.
"Well, why don't you know?" the judge insisted.
"It's none of my business."

His Honour's desk was a mess. All his files were splayed over his pedestal and he had still not identified which case it was. Furthermore, he had detected a certain arrogance in my tone which he didn't like one bit. The truth was I had become cocky. The courts and their jargon and hangers-on and little rituals meant nothing to me. I didn't shake and sweat like I had in the early days. I was no longer the perspiring, bright red wreck. In fact, it amused me now to watch the pomp and circumstance from these twits in the legal profession. Really, the entire edifice of this most noble of professions was built on one undeniable talent — the ability to read. If you boiled lawyers down to their essence that was all they did — they could read something and say, 'I think it means this.' And yet the behaviour of most, but not all of the legal profession, including judges, was extraordinary. It was as if they possessed powers divine.

There was still no sign of Julian or Lurie and into my head popped a vision of Julian in a sniper's nest outside the Lavender Bay boarding house with Lurie in the cross-hairs. "Surely not," I said to myself. "He must realise I was only joking about the hit man."

Judge Snarl looked up from the mess in front of him. "What's your name?"

"Alan," I replied, which could be my first or second name and as the judge was searching for a file with the word 'Alan' on it I added, "Phillip."

"Oh, right." The judge carried on thrashing through his papers.

"James," I added contemptuously.

One of the clerks rolled his eyes and called out, "It is Manly, your Honour. Mr Manly."

The judge was ready to explode. "There's nothing here about Manly."

"I am another," I said cryptically, fanning the flames.

"What? Who?"
"Another. As in 'Anor'."
"Here it is," cried the clerk with joy. "Lurie versus Day & Anor."

In an earlier era Judge Snarl would have had me hung, drawn and quartered. He was steaming by this stage and about a whisker away from locking me up for contempt of court. I could see the windsock blowing that way, but I didn't care. They didn't give a damn about me or what they did to my life and I'd had enough of the bullshit rhetoric and the phoney system they had. Julian arrived, much to my relief, and plonked his briefcase on the bar table. He muttered an apology and took a seat.
"Your Honour, my co-defendant, Mr Julian Day."

When I looked across I noticed Julian was his usual calm, unflustered self. Then the unspeakable thought flashed through my mind that if Julian had killed Lurie he would arrive at court looking exactly like this. Judge Snarl cleared his throat. "Righto. Manly, you say. Well, Mr Manly, why are you here?"
I couldn't resist the temptation. I slowly stood up and announced, "Your Honour, I am here because I have a document that says I should be here. Thus I am here." And then I sat down.
"What document?"
"This one," I replied, holding up the subpoena. "It says I am ordered to appear in this court on this date at this time before this judge, and here I am, happy to assist."

"Are you sure?"
"Oh yes, who wouldn't be thrilled to be here today?"
"I meant, are you sure you're meant to be in this court?"
"The listing says it is here today, I assume it is. You have my file."

At this point Lurie walked in and set himself up behind the bar table. For once I was glad to see him and even flashed him a smile. I was determined to enjoy myself. "This is the plaintiff, your Honour, Mr Lurie."
"Very good," the judge replied. "You're late."
"Yes, my sincere apologies to the court," grovelled Lurie. "There was a snap strike by the ferry crews."
"Very well."

Lurie then busied himself with his papers. We all waited as we had so often before. This was justice as it really was, the absolute opposite of the riveting, exciting law you see on television. There was no withering cross-examination from hot young lawyers, no witty exchanges between bench and bar, and no volte-face explosive evidence from glamorous witnesses with big tits. No courtroom I ever sat in was anything like that and I had by this stage clocked up hundreds of appearances. I'd seen more vigour and passion standing in line at the motor registry office. There is no packed public gallery with partisan supporters hanging on every word of evidence. People take forever to get to the point. There is an endless amount of time spent passing documents back and forth, back and forth — "I'm sorry I'm missing page two" — and interminable delays while one side waits for the other. I once calculated that I had spent more time in close quarters with Lurie than any other person. Well, I'd had enough of all this.

"Your Honour, while we're waiting for my un-learned friend here, things are a tad tight at the moment. I was wondering if you would you be so kind as to stake me for a loan?" Judge Snarl was dumbstruck. I pushed on. "Say, $40,000?"

The judge had found his voice. "What on earth are you raving about?"

"A loan, $40,000, to fund our defence."

"That's ridiculous," said the judge with a bit of a chuckle to himself. "This is a court of law, Mr Manly, not a bank. We don't loan money."

"I thought you'd say that." Then I turned and pointed a finger at the loathsome piece of shit on my left. "Could Your Honour then explain how it is that Mr Lurie was the beneficiary of your generosity?"

"You're not making any sense," the judge replied.

"Mr Lurie owes the Federal Court over $40,000."

"Nonsense."

"He has accrued a debt of $40,000 in outstanding filing fees."

The judge looked around and one of the court officials nodded his head ever so slightly.

Judge Snarl smiled. "I see where you're coming from, Mr Manly, but you have it all wrong."

"How so?"

"Well, to start with, this has nothing to do with me."

"I disagree," I shot back, interrupting the judge. "This has everything to do with you. You, Your Honour, are a representative of the Federal Court."

The judge looked down on me with a condescending sneer and cleared his throat. "Perhaps, Mr Manly, you should give up defending yourself."

"Why?"

"Because, and it's not my place to say this, but someone has to say it, it seems to me that you are taking this too personally, and being a little emotional, don't you think?"

"This man is destroying my life and you think I'm becoming emotional?" I replied as reasonably as I could.

"If the plaintiff's filing fees have been waived, you would need to take it up with the Registrar of the Court. But I'll save you the time because the Registrar would doubtless explain that this man is unemployed, hence the waiving of fees. I rest my case," the judge concluded, looking very pleased with himself.

"That's not possible, I'm afraid." I explained to the judge that I had already discussed the situation with the registry staff, who revealed that not only had they exempted him from paying filing fees without verifying that he was unemployed, but Lurie didn't even sign his own application requesting the waiving of fees. "Ipso facto," I went on, reverting to the Latin, perhaps the only Latin I knew, "the Federal Court is underwriting Lurie's legal action."

Judge Snarl stirred into action. "He is not being underwritten …"

"… and you gave him the money."

"I won't even dignify that nonsense with a response," the judge said angrily, and then went on to do precisely that. "It is the Parliament of the Commonwealth you have a complaint with, not the court. Take it to the Executive Government. Don't bring it to me."

Niggling him further I said, "No one gives me money to defend myself."

"I am not giving anybody money, Mr Manly."

"If only that was it, but I'm afraid it's a lot worse."

"This is all out of order. Sit down, please."

"No."

"I'm not listening to this rubbish. Sit down, Mr Manly."

"You see, this man," I stated, with finger and thumb cocked like a pistol aimed at Lurie, "this man, is a bankrupt."

Lurie jumped to his feet. "I am not a bankrupt."

"Mr Manly," the judge pleaded.

"He fought his bankruptcy all the way to the High Court of Australia and lost. This man is a bankrupt. Sad, but true. Now in this country it is a criminal offence to stand behind a bankrupt."

The judge roared, "Return to your seat, or I'll have you charged with contempt."

I waited a moment, locked eyes on the judge and then let him have it. "As I was saying, before I was rudely interrupted — by waiving this cretin's filing fees to the tune of $40,000, the Federal Court is standing behind a bankrupt. You are actually subsidising him to persist with his attack on me and Mr Day."

"Bailiff!" the judge called out. "Remove this man from the court."

"That's okay by me, I've finished now anyway," I said, even though I hadn't. I noticed the bailiff had puffed up his chest, but hadn't moved an inch. "My colleague, Julian Day, and I shall be initiating legal action against the Federal Court itself which is now a party to this action. Your Honour, I believe you will have to disqualify yourself from any further involvement in these proceedings on the basis that being an employee of the Federal Court you are an involved and interested party. Have a nice day."

Having said my piece I sat down and waited for the storm to come. I looked across to my adversary sitting there like a ghoul. I remembered my brother's assessment from years past that Lurie was a blackmailer. God knows, Julian and I were on the brink of exhaustion, but now we were at long last in control. Things were different now. We were different. When I thought back to when this all started I have to say I barely recognised the person I was. We had been a pair of undiscerning, hopeless greenhorns. Somehow, somewhere along the way Julian and I had come in to our own. Thanks to my Irish insanity genes and the determination of my British Bulldog friend, we realised we would survive this madness.

The courtroom was hushed. The judge stared at me and I stared back. Then, he took his glasses off, put them down and put them back on again. I realised his hand was shaking. The longer the silence ensued the more I knew we had them. When people start threatening to sue the court itself and have evidence to back up their allegations it's time to put the genie back in the bottle. Despite the precariousness of my present position, I knew we had won. The judge turned to the hapless bailiff and said in a world-weary voice, "Next case."

CHAPTER TWENTY-NINE

THE CONTRACT

At the very beginning it was agreed that Ava would be paid a bank interest rate of eight per cent, and when all monies owing were repaid in full, she would then transfer fifty per cent of the college over to me. The Australian College of Education was an incredible success and soon became one of the major education exporters in this country. Ava's cornerstone investment capital was totally repaid, with interest as agreed. However, when the moment arrived for her to transfer ownership, Ava had trouble remembering the details of our original agreement. When I explained the terms she said, "Why would I agree to that when I put all the money in?"

"That is true," I acknowledged, "but you will recall you have been paid interest and when the principal was repaid you were to transfer half the shares back to me."

When we had board meetings, Ava scrutinised every expenditure, no matter how small. It was amazing to watch. A couple of hundred dollars on couriers. Why couriers? Was it necessary? And yet at every monthly board meeting somehow Ava managed to avoid any discussion about the agreement to transfer the shares. Before the board meeting ended, I'd move my watch to the end of my wrist so I could see the time. Then, I would lay out my documents in order, fold my fingers and place

my hands on the table in front of me. Fingers folded, hands in front is very good in Asia. It's a very passive sort of a thing. At an opportune time, just as the board meeting was wrapping up and people were leaving, I would casually mention to Ava, "Have you had any time to think about the shares?"
"No," she'd reply, "I've been too busy this month."
"Okay."

The delay enraged my wife, Jennifer. "How did you go at your meeting today?" Being the eternal optimist, I never had a problem with Ava, but I would have to admit to Jennifer that actually nothing had happened at our meeting. I always knew that I had to be patient and wait. There are fifty-two cards in the pack. Ava played every card. You've got to wait for the last card to be played. Month after month this went on. Every time the subject came up the silences from Ava grew longer. At first when I mentioned it, she waited about a minute before replying, as cool as a cucumber, "Yes, I have to think about that." Then she'd leave. After about six months of this shadow play the silences from Ava, when this subject came up, were reaching three or four minutes. Eventually, at one of these discussions I politely mentioned to Ava there was a contract in writing regarding the transfer of ownership.
"A contract?" she said, sounding amazed.
"Yes, a contract that both you and I signed."
"Oh," she said nonchalantly, "I don't remember that. Have you a copy?"
I must confess that when she said that I did quietly shit myself.
"Yeah," I confirmed in a rather unconvincing manner.
"Good," she said and walked off.

I was sure this contract existed, but after so many years of drama and documents flying back and forth, the worry was that it had been lost. When I told my long-suffering wife what had happened she became immediately depressed. She was certain I would have lost the agreement with Ava and here we were going to be ripped off again, or worse, become once more embroiled in legal action.

The drive from my office at 1841 George Street to my home in the suburbs was one of the longest trips of my life. I was unbelievably stressed. If I couldn't find that document we'd be seriously fucked. The Australian College of Education had grown and now had a multi-million dollar turnover. The contract with Ava was worth a fortune. I pulled up in the driveway and walked into our home office. There before me was a row of filing cabinets, looking very similar to the layout of the filing cabinets I had searched in the Philippines for the missing company seal. This was a reassuring thought. I was 'he who see through steel'. I am an obsessive compulsive who keeps every document known to mankind. All the documents relating to all my business and other interests had been filed meticulously. Even so, I'm only human. Sometimes, things go astray.

I stood before the filing cabinets and thought for a moment. Then I slid out the first drawer which was chock-a-block full of court documents about Lurie. The second drawer was the same, as was the third. Then I creaked open the last drawer. Inside was a suspension folder labelled promisingly, 'Ava's Contract'. The file had bulldog clips all across the top. Inside that was a manila folder which had been stapled together. Written all over it in red ink was 'Ava's Contract'. I prised open the staples and inside there was a plastic sleeve and inside that the original contract with Ava's signature on it.

While I was closing the drawer a label marked 'Unpresented Cheque' caught my eye. I pulled it out and there inside the file was a handwritten cheque for $115.00 made out in favour of one E. Lurie. I'd forgotten that all those years ago Julian and I had caved in to his demands and given him a cheque for $115 to meet his photocopying expenses. In a fit of pique, Lurie had torn it up and stormed from the room. Being an obsessive compulsive I had picked up the cheque, taped it together and filed it away. If only Lurie had just put the cheque in his pocket and walked away. But, of course, Lurie always had bigger plans. Almost a decade later and it was still going on.

Telling Ava that I had found the contract made not the slightest difference. "Oh," she said feigning surprise, "you have found the agreement?"
"Yes."
"Okay."
At our next board meeting I brought the contract in with me. After the other board members had left I showed it to her. She took it and held it up to the light examining it with all the intensity of someone checking out counterfeit currency. "Is that really my signature?" she asked with complete innocence.
"It is," I confirmed. "See, it has your name underneath the signature."
Seven minutes. That's how long I waited for her next move.

ONE ONE FIVE

Have you ever sat there waiting for an answer for seven minutes? It's a long time. She was a woman who had very rarely been cornered in her life, but she knew at that moment I had her cold. Alan had played the last card and it was an ace. I watched the second hand of my watch. By now I was a master of doing business Asian style. Wait. Play the silence. Seven minutes later she said. "Yes, but I don't remember signing that."

"I was there, Ava, when you signed it."

"Well," she said at last, "I guess I'll have to give it to my solicitor and see what he thinks of it." As she started to scoop up the contract I quickly took it and slipped into her hands a photocopy. "Here's a copy," I explained.

It was a binding contract and even though her investment had turned into a little gold mine, this contract said she had to share the gold mine. I believe Ava was prepared to kill a cat that day, the cat's name being Alan.

Ava was an amazing person. However, as an Asian female, it was very hard for her to be taken seriously in Australia. To compensate for that she played the game of being inscrutable even harder, but all that did was put up a bigger barrier. The joy of being Asian and being inscrutable is that time is not such a big deal. In the West everything's in the timing. I'd go to meetings and Ava would sit there for half an hour and not move a single muscle. In Asia that was power, but in Sydney, Westerners misread her silence as lack of interest. Whereas Ava deliberately arrived late to enhance her status, this was interpreted as rudeness. She had problems relating to people and there were all these defence mechanisms which got in the way. Ava was trying to do business in the Australian culture, but the people on the other side of the table were not reading her at all. I think because of that she wasn't really all that successful in business in this country.

Although I had trumped her with the ace, now she wanted more. "Alan, you could allow another fifty thousand," she said in her calculatingly feminine way. The company couldn't really afford it, but the Asian hook was in there. Westerners often have trouble when it comes to contracts with Asian countries and companies. When we sign a contract, we think of it as a fixed, rigid agreement, but to the Asians, a contract is a living organism. Negotiations are always on the agenda and never really finish. In the silence, I looked into her eyes and understood what she was offering: "I'll get out of your life peacefully and forever, if you give me another fifty grand." I didn't need her as an enemy, so I agreed. After the last board meeting she rocked up with spray-on clothes looking like a million dollars. I handed her a cheque. "Ava, in accordance with your instructions, the cheque has been made out to cash." Not a smile, nothing.
She just looked at it and said, "Yes." The words 'thank you' did not pass her lips. She put the cheque back in the envelope and asked, "Will that be all?" She walked out past reception. She knew James, my son, of course, who was on reception that day. James had fetched and carried for Ava lots of times over the years. She turned on her heels and said, "Goodbye James," and walked out. I've never seen her since.

CHAPTER THIRTY

THE LAST TIME

The threat by Julian and me to take legal action against the Federal Court itself was the catalyst which precipitated the end. Over the course of close to ten years we had appeared before almost every judge of the District Court, the Supreme Court and the Federal Court. We had even been before Justice Gummow, Justice Callinan and Justice McHugh of the High Court. Our reputation as advocates had soared and we were starting to look very good on our feet. No one had ever taken a court to court in living memory and they knew we were not bluffing.

In August 2003, we were called before a judge in the Supreme Court whom I had never seen before. This was McGregor, J. He was very distinguished looking and held himself with such dignity I immediately felt great confidence in him. Judge McGregor had gravitas. He had a tipstaff and was surrounded by sheriffs. As he began reading his judgment, Lurie stood up.
"You're making a mistake," he wailed.
"Please take your seat, Mr Lurie," the judge asked ever so politely, "while I go on with my finding."

Lurie returned to his seat at the bar table beside us. Looking at Lurie, I remembered that years before his actions had reminded me of the cartoon character, Coyote. For those too young to know these things, a very popular cartoon at the cinema when I was a boy was the Road Runner and Coyote. The Road Runner was a smiling blue bird, like an ostrich, who travelled at great speed along these open desert highways in America. His nemesis was the Coyote, a sad-sack desperado whose only goal in life was to destroy the Road Runner. Why he actually wanted to do this I can't remember. Perhaps it was never explained, or maybe he simply wished to eat the Road Runner. Each cartoon had an identical plot — Coyote would spend hours if not days erecting an elaborate explosive device to wipe out the Road Runner — but at the critical moment something would go horribly wrong and instead Coyote would explode in flames as the Road Runner roared by making his inane cry of "Beep beep."

As a child I watched these cartoons at the movies and the mob around me roared with laughter at the success of the Road Runner and the idiocy of the Coyote. Perhaps this is where my contrariness began. I could not but admire the Coyote. For me the Road Runner was shallow and superficial. He was a one-trick pony. Speed. He ran fast and that was it, whereas my hero, Coyote, was devious, ingenious and creative. But best of all he never ever gave up. Even though at the end of every episode he only succeeded in blowing himself to smithereens, he miraculously survived, albeit in tatters, yet he never gave up. With each episode the explosive devices Coyote designed became even more elaborate and ingenious, but all to the same sad end.

And so it was with Lurie. The man kept dreaming up yet more

ingenious legal ambushes to destroy us and at every single turn they blew up in his face. However, there was never any sympathy in my heart for the Coyote I confronted in the courtrooms. His own goals were not funny, but sad and sick at heart. I think he had long ago realised that he could not beat us legally and so could only win by waging a campaign of mutually assured destruction. Obviously, this was not a dispute over $115, or the District Court case that he lost costing him $40,000, or over any of the other thirty plus court cases he started. It wasn't about any amount of money. This was a war and had been all along. This was a war which was fought in the courtrooms of Sydney. It consumed our lives and certainly came close to destroying our careers, our livelihoods, and our families. When he knew he couldn't win, Lurie pushed us to the edge physically and psychologically. He was desperate for Julian and me to turn on each other, or to suffer a nervous collapse, or deflect us from our business interests so we would fall into financial ruin. And yet, like all swindlers, Lurie was also trapped. He seemed pathologically incapable of giving up.

Like the Coyote character, Lurie seemed indestructible whereas Julian and I, riddled with self-doubt, with personal relationships in ruins, were the ones who endured all manner of crises. The endless anxiety, the acute pain and the desperate loneliness of this fight took its toll. "Why is this happening to me? Why do I bother?" I would ask myself. I don't know if I ever knew the answer to that question.

Judge McGregor went on reading his judgment which ripped Lurie into small pieces. McGregor found that Lurie had failed to demonstrate any error on the part of any magistrate or judge in all the proceedings he had initiated. Every appeal had been dismissed. His Statements of Claim were incoherent, confused, obscure and flawed. He had been convicted of assaulting one of the defendants and was declared a bankrupt for failing to pay costs awarded to the defendants.

"This is like going back to the Rum Corps," Lurie interjected.

"I would ask you to be temperate in your remarks," the judge shot back and resumed reading his judgment. He had come to the view that there was no sustainable cause of action in the Statement of Claim and that the proceedings were at an end. "It is appropriate to dismiss the Statement of Claim and I so order," the judge declared.

Lurie stood up, defiant to the end. "Obviously, I am going to appeal your decision."

The judge threw Lurie a withering look and said, "This case is dismissed. Do you understand me, Mr Lurie. The cause has come to an end. I want you to tell me you understand what I am saying."

Finally, we had a judge with balls.

Lurie stood there stunned. The judge repeated his remark and still Lurie said nothing. "Do you understand me?"

After what seemed a life time Lurie mumbled, "I understand, your Honour."

"Never, ever again," warned the judge. "You hear me. You cannot commence legal action in this state. I have directed the Registrar not to accept the filing of any document intended to initiate proceedings in this court by or on behalf of E.E. Lurie without the prior leave of a judge of this court. You are not to file any more documents in a NSW court. If you do I will have you arrested and imprisoned." Bang went the gavel, like a full stop at the end of an awfully long sentence. It was all over.

That day when I drove home I shot a quick look across at the letterbox as I nudged up the driveway. It was empty. Maybe, it really was the end. The next day there were nothing but bills in the mail. Never was a man so pleased to see bills. And so it went on. After about a week of this I rang Julian. "Anything?" I asked. He didn't need me to explain further. He knew exactly what I was thinking. "As quiet as the grave," was his happy reply.

Two adventurous young men recently paddled a kayak from Australia to New Zealand. A gruelling, unrelenting battle against the elements to go where none have gone before. This is what it felt like for Julian and me, except with some significant differences. Apart from the obvious fact that neither Julian nor I are young, athletic or handsome, those young men chose to paddle across the Tasman. They knew where they were going, when they would arrive and if they did this they would become famous for their achievement. Whereas podgy, Pommie Julian and I, his hyperactive obsessive compulsive Aussie side-kick Ratso, found themselves one day adrift in the legal waters off Cape Horne without any paddles, or to use the vernacular, up shit creek in a barbed wire canoe. Julian and I were not just defendants in various vexatious legal suits. There was always another dimension to this conflict. This had been a war, a cold war and a dirty war. We were like two citizen soldiers press-ganged to fight in a foreign land without weapons. It was all hand-to-hand combat. We might not have had God on our side, but we were convinced that our cause was just. For Julian and me this was not ultimately about those grand ideals of liberty, justice and truth; all we were after was our freedom. We just wanted the war to be over so we could go home. In hindsight some wars can seem to have been all for nothing, but I never felt like that. We never had a choice. Had Lurie succeeded the outcome would have been horrific. When a man comes face to face with pure evil, he must draw a line in the sand and make a stand.

We had little idea what we were doing, not a clue where we were going, or when it would ever end. It took ten of the best years of our lives, and when our kayak finally reached the end, the bitter end, there were no cheering crowds, no entries into record books, no chat show celebrity, no book and movie deals. Instead, this fabulous nobody went home and mowed the lawn, and my partner pulled himself up on a stool at the pub and flirted with the barmaids. Nonetheless, I felt that our achievement had been remarkable.

Together the pair of us had set off into the unknown with not a day's legal training and on our own appeared before every court jurisdiction in the country and won. When I sat down and calculated the time Julian and I spent in the Sydney court precinct working on these cases the legal bill alone would have been over half a million dollars. And never in that decade did we receive one red cent from Lurie despite winning numerous judgments against him. If there hadn't been two of us, neither would have succeeded. Julian persevered where many would have thrown up their hands and walked away. There was loyalty and trust between us from the beginning. A couple of times Lurie tried to split the opposition, but soon realised there was no joy to be had there.

With every passing day and not a writ in sight, I was beginning to feel jubilant. But just when you think it's safe to go back into the water, the unexpected happens. At a barbeque I was explaining, or more probably, bragging about the fact that over a twelve year period, I made over two hundred and forty court appearances at the Magistrate's Court, the District Court, the Supreme Court, the Federal Court as well as the High Court. A favourite niece, someone clever, compassionate and rational looked at me in horror and exclaimed, "Oh Uncle Alan, whatever did you do?" I walked away and cried.

Whatever did happen to Elliott Elias Lurie? Well you may ask. Being cursed with a brain which never switches off I don't sleep at night, but nap in between reading, watching television or surfing the internet. In the middle of one such night I found myself watching replays of the day's news on one of the cable networks. One of the big news stories of 2003 was the Howard government's push for a free trade agreement with the Americans.

Public submissions made in hearings before the Australian Senate were televised and there before this senate committee was a man, a rather bland, forgettable-looking man, inoffensive, well presented albeit in a cheap suit holding forth on the intricacies and complexities of negotiating with the great nation of America. I'd know him anywhere, of course. We spent ten years glaring at each other across the trenches of the Federal Court. You had to give it to him. He was as brilliant as he was diabolical. Tears streamed down my face and yet I was laughing. My emotions were so confused it was impossible for me to know if I was deliriously happy or crying in despair. I watched in awe as Lurie, convicted fraudster, undischarged bankrupt, bully and thug had the senators enthralled as he explained his submission. I knew then that it really was all over, that I had my life back.

Made in the USA
Monee, IL
13 September 2026

62981006R00164